Bounce Back from BANKRUPTCY

Third Edition

A Step-By-Step Guide to Getting Back on Your Financial Feet

By Paula Langguth Ryan

Pellingham Casper Communications, LLC
How-To Publications That Make A Difference
1121 Annapolis Road, Suite 120
Odenton, MD 21113

Publisher's Cataloging-in-Publication
(Provided by Quality Books, Inc.)
Ryan, Paula Langguth.
Bounce back from bankruptcy : a step-by-step guide to getting
back on your financial feet / by Paula Langguth Ryan.
— 3rd ed.
p. cm.
ISBN 1-889605-02-6
1. Bankruptcy — United States — Popular works.
2. Finance, Personal. I. Title
KF1524.6.R93 2001   346.73'078
                                 QBI01-301

Pellingham Casper books are available for special promotions and
premiums. For details, contact: Director, Special Markets,
800/507-9244

Third Edition — 2001

Printed in the United States of America

Cover Photo By Steven Anderson

Table of Contents

<u>Dedication</u>

To my father, Wayne Langguth,
and to my friend and former literary agent,
Robert Drake.
Their personal triumphs over physical traumas
remind me every day that
money isn't everything.

Acknowledgments

A lot of heart and soul went into the creation of this book, and not all of it was mine. Once again, I am eternally grateful to a number of people without whose love, laughter, support, gruntwork and understanding this latest edition would have remained a dream. I offer my heartfelt thanks to these people who fed me, literally and spiritually over the past months: Refik Agri, Herbert Beskin, Patrick Brawner, Mary Byrd Brown, Mary Sheppard Burton, Linda Damesyn, Ken and Daria Dolan, Daria Finn, Jennifer Gaillard, Sharon Gorenstein, Janet L. Hall, Daphne Hull, Kate Hull, Beth Kaufman, Rebecca Langguth, Nellie Lauth, April J. May, Ronda McCullough-Clark, Mike McFeely, Luanne McKenna, Kathy Miller and Ted Zeiders.

Several people directly involved with this project deserve special thanks, including cover designer Tracy Anadale, whose crackerjack graphic arts skills were always available at a moment's notice; photographer Steven Anderson, who always makes me look good; and Michelle Simari, without whose unending support during the creation of the first edition, this book would not exist.

I also offer thanks to everyone who tithed to me this year, everyone who has ever contemplated bankruptcy protection, and the thousands of kindred spirits who have posted messages on **America On-Line's** *Moneywhiz* and *theWhiz.com* personal finance forums, attended my on-line *Credit & Debt 101* and *Prosperity* classes and my real life *Break the Debt Cycle — For Good!* and *Bounce Back From Bankruptcy* seminars or subscribed to my e-zine, *The Art of Abundance*. I thank you all for your strength and courage.

A special thanks to my dear friend, spiritual mentor and intuitive counselor, Nellie Lauth. I am forever enhanced by the growth you help me make.

Finally, I am compelled to single out one person for special mention and that is Janet L. Hall, mentor, motivator and professional organizer extraordinarie — for believing in my vision from the beginning, and for always being my friend.

Thank you all for being exactly who you are!

Forward to the Third Edition

I put off writing a third edition of this book for a year, waiting to see what effect pending bankruptcy reform would have on the strategies I share with you in these pages. Weeks turned into months, and then years, as Congress debated whether or not to pass a very creditor-friendly bankruptcy reform.

Not content to sit idly by, I testified before the National Bankruptcy Review Commission, explaining why I thought Congress' proposals would do more harm than good for hard-working Americans who were already struggling financially. I finally came to believe that good will prevail and that bankruptcy reform will not pass until and unless it is more even-handed, offering consumers as many protections as it does creditors.

My editor and others close to my work have convinced me that even if a future bill passes, ninety percent of the information in this book will always be applicable, because these are sound strategies that are not reliant on any legislation. This edition contains countless updates and additional motivating information, all of which is designed to help you to start taking control of your finances.

The highest compliment my readers have given me is when they tell me they wish they'd had a copy of this book before they declared bankruptcy.

If you have a loved one who is having financial troubles, please share this book with them, before things get worse. Working together, I believe we can all be empowered to make good financial choices that will bring us financial freedom instead of keeping us slaves to MasterCard and other creditors.

I originally wrote *Bounce Back From Bankruptcy* because my friend Michele was going through bankruptcy and was filled with questions. She knew I'd gone bankrupt and come out the other end, able to buy a home, buy a car and get a new credit card, all at reasonable interest rates. How did I do it?

I'd discovered something that many other people have overlooked: Bankruptcy doesn't mean you have to pay higher interest rates on the credit you receive — it just means that you have to shop around a bit more to find someone willing to lend you money at the going interest rates.

The first edition contained information based on my experience rebuilding my credit and from interviews with many financial professionals. The second edition contained several new chapters, including Breaking The Debt Cycle —For Good!, Easing Job Fears After Bankruptcy, Renting An Apartment or House After Bankruptcy, and How To Travel Without Credit as well as expanded What If You Find Yourself In Over Your Head Again? and Keep Up The Good Work sections.

I hope this book helps you get out of debt, break your personal debt cycle and achieve the life of your dreams. I'm devoted to giving you the resources you need to change the way you think and feel about money — so you may achieve presonal prosperity and abundance in all areas of your life. Please write and let me know how well I succeed!

Paula Langguth Ryan
1121 Annapolis Road, Suite 120
Odenton, MD 21113
PaulaRyan@ArtOfAbundance.com

introduction

Bankruptcy Is Not the End of the Road

I am living proof that bankruptcy is not the end of the road. In fact, it can actually be the beginning of a brand new start! Whether or not you ever want to see a credit card again is up to you. But sooner or later, you may need to get a car loan, or you may want to buy a home. The step-by-step strategies in this book will help you get the best possible loan or mortgage, regardless of your past mistakes.

You *can* get a credit card, a car loan, and even become a homeowner after declaring bankruptcy. Bankruptcy is *not* a ten-year mistake, as some people would have you believe. My bankruptcy was still on my credit reports when I accomplished all these goals — without paying higher interest rates.

My bankruptcy was finalized in 1988. By 1989, I had a new credit card, in my name alone. In 1993, I was able to get a $6,000 car loan (at a reasonable 9% interest rate) and bought a used Honda. Finally, in 1994 — less than six years after I declared bankruptcy, I bought my very first home.

Many stumbling blocks tripped me up along the way. I could have avoided these obstacles — and rebuilt my credit much sooner — if someone had been able to show me the right way to get back on my feet. That's why I decided to take what I had learned and share it with others.

Step-by-step, this book will show you how to get back on a firm financial footing, put your bankruptcy behind you and live debt-free. I hope you will use these strategies as a springboard to a new, more financially secure life.

These strategies have worked for me and for thousands of other Americans who have declared bankruptcy. In fact, my sister-in-law followed the steps in this book and bought her first home, a huge Victorian, one year after bankruptcy.

Now you too can put these strategies to work for you. You don't need to waste all the time that I did, running around in circles, trying to rebuild your credit or running yourself back into debt again.

Once I declared bankruptcy and started to rebuild my credit, it wasn't long before I found myself in trouble again. I had the best intentions to live within my means. But offers of "easy credit" were appealing and one thing led to another until I found myself carrying debt from month to month again.

I knew I needed to break the debt cycle, so I started looking for ways to change my lifelong money habits. Along the way, I discovered that the best way to change how I dealt with money was to first change the way I *thought* about money.

I was amazed at the difference in my life, once I started changing my attitudes about debt and money. You, too, will be amazed at how easy it is to stay out of debt and start building real prosperity for yourself and your family. You can start rebuilding your credit and changing your attitudes about money, right now. So what are you waiting for?

Turn the page and let's get started on your new financial future!

chapter 1

Taking the First Step Toward Rebuilding Your Credit

Your credit problems are now a thing of the past, whether your bankruptcy was a Chapter 7 or Chapter 13.

Even so, you may find that creditors still turn you down, because of problems that show up on your credit report — even if the problem occurred as many as ten years ago. So don't be discouraged. Your first step once your bankruptcy has been discharged is to check all of your credit reports.

Creditors use your credit report to determine how safe a credit risk you are. Luckily, bankruptcy doesn't automatically make you a bad credit risk. In fact, as long as all your other credit information is good, bankruptcy can actually make getting credit easier. That's because you can only declare bankruptcy once every seven years. So, you're much less likely to default on a creditor.

There are ways you can re-establish yourself as a good credit risk, no matter what your credit history may be. But you need to see what your creditors see about your bill-paying habits. And, even more important, you need to make sure the information in your credit report is correct.

Getting Copies of Your Credit Reports

You have the right to know what is in your credit reports. There are three major credit bureaus (CBI/Equifax, Experian, and TransUnion), plus many smaller regional and local ones. If there are no local credit bureaus listed in your phone book, call your bank or a local department store and ask for the name of your regional credit bureau. Anytime you are denied credit, you can find out — for free — what's in the credit report which that creditor used. You can also get a free copy of your credit report twice a year from credit bureaus if you live in Georgia, and once a year if you live in Colorado, Maryland, Massachusetts, New Jersey or Vermont, whether or not you've been denied credit.

All other states charge a processing fee. The fee is capped at $2 for Maine, $3 for Minnesota, $5.30 for Connecticut and $8.50 for all other states. A second annual report costs Maryland residents $5.25 and Vermont residents $7.50. For everyone else, extra credit reports cost $8. Believe me, this will be the most worthwhile $15-$25.50 investment you will ever make in your financial future!

You might be tempted to use a credit report compiling company like Credco, which merges information from all your credit reports. I don't recommend doing this, for one important reason. When you merge all three credit reports, especially if there are any errors, all you get is one big mess. You'll wind up with a summary page loaded with incorrect information that will take you weeks to sort out — if you can sort it out at all. Instead of getting a complied report, go ahead and get each individual credit report. Then clear up any errors, one report at a time.

When a creditor denies you credit based on information from your credit report, that creditor must give you the name and address of the credit bureau where they got your report. If you've recently been turned down for credit, start by asking for a copy of your credit report from that credit bureau, since you won't have to pay for it, no matter what.

Even if you have not been denied credit recently, you should still order a copy of your credit report from each credit bureau, so you can see what potential creditors see when they consider you for credit, such as a car loan or a mortgage.

Getting Your Experian Credit Report

If you have been denied credit in the last 60 days you can get a free copy of your Experian credit report by calling 888-397-3742. If you prefer to send a letter, I recommend using the following letter to Experian. Be sure to attach a copy of the letter from your potential creditor that shows you were denied credit based on your credit report.

(Date)

Experian
Attn.: NCAC
PO Box 2002
Allen, TX 75013

Dear Sir/Madam:

I am writing to request a copy of my credit report. I was denied credit by [name of creditor who denied you credit] on [date you were denied credit] based on information in my credit report.

As requested, I am providing my personal information.

- *First Name, Middle Initial, Last Name (+ Jr., Sr., II, III, IV if applicable)*
- *Spouse's First Name*
- *Present Home Address, including any apartment number, and zip code*
- *Previous Home Addresses for the Past 5 Years, including any apartment numbers, and zip codes*
- *Social Security Number*
- *Date of Birth*

Also attached is a copy of the declination letter from [creditor's name]. I thank you in advance for your help in this matter.

Sincerely,

[Your name]

You should receive your credit report three to four weeks after you send the letter.

If you live in a state that allows you to get a free copy of your credit report every year, you can order your credit report over the phone by calling 888-397-3742 or you can send the following letter to Experian requesting a copy of your credit report:

(Date)

Experian
PO Box 9595
Allen, TX 75013-0036

Dear Sir/Madam:

I am writing to request a complimentary copy of my credit report.

As requested, I am providing my personal information.

- *First Name, Middle Initial, Last Name (+ Jr., Sr., II, III, IV if applicable)*
- *Spouse's First Name*
- *Present Home Address, including any apartment number and zip code*
- *Previous Home Addresses for the Past 5 Years, including any apartment numbers and zip codes*
- *Social Security Number*
- *Date of Birth*

Also attached is a copy of my latest [creditor billing statement, utility bill or driver's license] verifying my current address. I thank you in advance for your help in this matter.

Sincerely,

[Your Name]

You must include the personal information listed in the letter, and proof of your current address. A copy of your utility bill, billing statement or driver's license will do the trick.

If you need to pay for a copy of your credit report, you can order it on-line by visiting http://www.experian.com. Of course, you can also order your free report on-line, but you must be willing to give out your credit/debit card information. Before you give out your credit card number over the Internet, check to make sure you're on a secured site. If the site doesn't specifically state that you will be making a secure transaction, I'd recommend giving them your credit card information over the phone. You're going to be working very hard to rebuild your credit — I don't want credit card fraud to get in your way.

If you prefer to deal with the U.S. mail, send the following letter to Experian requesting a copy of your credit report:

(Date)

Experian
PO Box 2104
Allen, TX 75013-2104

Dear Sir/Madam:

I am writing to request a copy of my credit report.

As requested, I am providing my personal information, and any necessary fee.

- *First Name, Middle Initial, Last Name (+ Jr., Sr., II, III, if applicable)*
- *Spouse's First Name*
- *Present Home Address, including any apartment number and zip code*
- *Previous Home Addresses for the Past 5 Years, including any apartment numbers and zip codes*
- *Social Security Number*
- *Date of Birth*

Also attached is a copy of my latest [creditor billing statement, utility bill or driver's license] verifying my current address. I thank you in advance for your help in this matter.

Sincerely,

[Your Name]

You must include the personal information listed in the letter, and proof of your current address. A copy of your utility bill, billing statement or driver's license will do the trick.

Getting Your CBI/Equifax Report

Depending on where you live, creditors may refer to a credit bureau known as CBI or Equifax. Both names refer to the same company, which I'll call CBI/Equifax to keep things simple. Requesting your CBI/Equifax credit report is less formal than it is at other credit bureaus. You can request your CBI/Equifax credit report by mail, fax, telephone — even over the Internet.

To order (and even view!) your CBI/Equifax credit report on-line, you'll need a credit or debit card. Simply go to their website at http://www.credit.equifax.com and follow the instructions for ordering your CBI/Equifax credit report. You should receive your credit report in 2-3 weeks.

The quickest way to order your credit report by phone is to call the CBI/Equifax automated phone line at 800/997-2493.

If you were *not* denied credit in the past 60 days, and you live outside Colorado, Georgia, Maryland, Massachusetts, New Jersey and Vermont, you'll need a credit card to order your report by phone. When you call the automated phone line, an automated voice will ask you a few personal questions, including your Social Security number. If you don't know your Social Security number off the top of your head, grab your Social Security card before you call. Your answers will be recorded, and you'll receive your credit report in 4-6 weeks. If you've recently moved, the automated system may not have your current address on file. In this case, you'll need to order your CBI/Equifax credit report by mail.

To order your credit report by mail, send the following letter — along with any required check — to CBI/Equifax:

(Date)

CBI/Equifax
PO Box 105252
Atlanta, GA 30348-5252

Dear Sir/Madam:

I am writing to request a copy of my credit report. As requested, I am providing my personal information and any necessary fee.

- *First Name, Middle Initial, Last Name (+ Jr., Sr., II, III, IV if applicable)*
- *Spouse's First Name*
- *Present Home Address, including zip code*
- *Previous Addresses for the Past 5 Years, including zip codes*
- *Social Security Number*
- *Date of Birth*

Also attached is a copy of my latest [utility bill or driver's license] verifying my current address. I thank you in advance for your help in this matter.

Sincerely,

[Your Name]

If you have been denied credit, send the following letter to CBI/Equifax. Attach to it a copy of the letter from your potential creditor that shows you were denied credit based on your report.

(Date)

CBI/Equifax
PO Box 105873
Atlanta, GA 30348-5873

Dear Sir/Madam:

I am writing to request a copy of my credit report. I was denied credit by [name of creditor who denied you credit] on [date you were denied credit] based on information in my credit report.

As requested, I am providing my personal information.

> • *First Name, Middle Initial, Last Name (+ Jr., Sr., II, III, IV if applicable)*
> • *Spouse's First Name*
> • *Present Home Address, including zip code*
> • *Previous Home Addresses for the Past 5 Years, including zip codes*
> • *Social Security Number*
> • *Date of Birth*
>
> *Also attached is a copy of the declination letter from [creditor's name] and a copy of my latest [utility bill or drivers license], verifying my current address. I thank you in advance for your help in this matter.*
>
> *Sincerely,*
>
> *[Your Name]*

If you won't owe a fee, you can fax either letter to CBI/ Equifax at 770/375-3150, for speedier service.

Getting Your TransUnion Credit Report

If you live in a state that doesn't charge for a credit report or you've been denied credit in the last 60 days by a creditor who has used TransUnion's credit report, you can easily request your TransUnion credit report by telephone.

Call the TransUnion Credit Report Request Line at 800/ 888-4213 and follow the automated instructions. You'll tape record answers to nine questions about your general personal information, including your Social Security number and your previous addresses for the last two years. The phone call takes about ten minutes.

If you haven't been denied credit recently or you live in a state that charges a fee, you'll need to request your TransUnion credit report by mail. Send the following letter, plus your fee, to TransUnion.

(Date)

TransUnion
PO Box 390
Springfield, PA 19064-0390

Dear Sir/Madam:

I am writing to request a copy of my credit report. As requested, I am providing my personal information and any necessary fee.

- *First Name, Middle Initial, Last Name (+ Jr., Sr., II, III, IV if applicable)*
  - *Spouse's First Name*
  - *Present Home Address, including zip code*
  - *Previous Home Addresses for the Past 5 Years, including zip codes*
  - *Social Security Number*
  - *Date of Birth*

Also attached is a copy of my latest [utility bill or driver's license] verifying my current address. I thank you in advance for your help in this matter.

Sincerely,

[Your Name]

Once your credit reports arrive in the mail you'll be another step closer to your goal of financial security. The next step is to find out exactly what your credit report says about your credit history — and your credit worthiness.

What Your Credit Report Says About You

Your credit report contains a list of many of your current and past creditors, how much you borrowed from them, and whether you paid your bills on time. It should also confirm that your bankruptcy has been discharged, and list any outstanding liens or judgments against you.

Most creditors only report information to credit bureaus when your account becomes 90 days or more past due, or if your account is sent to a collection agency. Other creditors report information to the credit bureaus every month, so your payment history on those accounts will be very detailed.

Almost all creditors will list your payment history in 30 day increments. Your credit report will show how many times you paid 30, 60, 90, or 120 days late. To show all this information, most credit bureaus use a coding system that is explained on the back of your credit report.

Basically, your accounts will be listed as "R" for revolving credit, "I" for installment loans, or "O" for open-end loan, followed by a number that tells whether you paid on time or late. An "R-1" for example, refers to a revolving loan that you "paid as agreed," "R-2" means you "paid in more than 30 days, but no more than 60 days," etc. (up to "R-5," which means "paid in more than 120 days"). An "R-9" means the account has been charged off as an unpaid debt.   Once your bankruptcy is discharged, you can start improving your credit report by bringing all remaining accounts up-to-date and continuing to pay on time.

It's important that you understand every piece of information on your credit report. Otherwise, you could wind up overlooking something that is important to a future creditor — and you could wind up getting turned down for a car loan or mortgage because of an error on your credit report. I don't want to see that happen. So, if anything is unclear, call the credit bureau at the number listed on your credit report and ask a representative to walk you through the information.

What You Need To Look At First

When you look at your credit report, there are two basic places where obvious errors commonly occur — incorrect personal information or out-of-date information.

1. *Incorrect personal information.* I know it might seem silly, but most errors are very simple errors in your personal information. Start by checking your personal information to make sure it's correct. Verify your name, address, Social Security number, and employment information. Next, make sure all the accounts listed actually belong to you. If you have a common name, or are a Jr., Sr. or II, etc., you may have information in your credit report that belongs to someone else.

2. *Out-of-date information.* Many other errors occur when old information is left on your credit report. For the most part, negative (and correctly reported) information that is more than seven years old must automatically be removed. Here are the exceptions:

• Chapter 7 bankruptcies remain for ten years.

• Chapter 13 bankruptcies stay on for seven years from the date you *complete* your repayment plan.

• Tax liens, paid lawsuits and judgments stay on seven years from the date you paid them off.

• Unpaid lawsuits or judgments will stay listed on your credit report for seven years from the date they were entered or the time allowed by law for collecting the judgment, whichever is longer. This period of time varies from state to state, but it can be as long as 20 years.

To find out how long an unpaid lawsuit or judgment can stay on your credit report, contact your State Attorney General's Office (which you can find in the blue pages of your telephone book) and ask what the "statute of limitations" is for unpaid lawsuits. If the statute of limitations is longer than seven years, that's how long it will take for the unpaid lawsuit or judgment to fall off your credit report.

Once you've corrected all of these obvious errors, it's time to take a look at your credit report with a more critical eye — to see what other information is being reported in error. The first place to start after your bankruptcy is discharged is with the accounts that were included in your bankruptcy.

Updating Your Discharged Accounts

When you're correcting your credit reports, it's vital that you update the way your discharged accounts are listed. Sit down with your bankruptcy paperwork and compare your discharged debts to the debts that are listed on your credit report. Check off each item on your bankruptcy papers as you look for it on your credit report. You should find these debts listed on your credit report as "discharged under bankruptcy protection," or, "reorganized under Chapter 13 bankruptcy."

If these debts are still listed as delinquent accounts, under collection, or charged off, your creditor may not have notified the credit bureau that their debt was included in your bankruptcy. Sometimes this information just falls through the cracks. Luckily, updating it and removing the now incorrect delinquency is pretty easy. Start by making multiple copies of your bankruptcy paperwork. You'll need copies of your listed debts (Schedules D, E and F), and copies of your notice of discharge (Order of Discharge).

Next, you'll need to send a letter to the credit bureau pointing out each account that continues to appear delinquent. For example, my CBI/Equifax credit report showed that I still had an outstanding car loan — and that the creditor had slapped me with a lien. But my car loan had been listed — and discharged — under my bankruptcy.

What seemed like a big problem actually had an easy solution. Use the following letter to update your negative information and wipe your slate clean of this incorrect information.

The following letter was all it took to get the incorrect information off my credit report.

(Date)

[Credit Bureau]
[Address]
[City, State, Zip]
Re: [Your Social Security Number and/or Account Number]

Dear Sir/Madam:

My credit report shows that the following account is [status of account as it currently appears on your credit report].

Enclosed is a copy of my listed debts and my final discharge papers which show that this account was discharged under my bankruptcy on [date of final discharge].

Please update your records to show this change and send me a letter indicating that this change was made.

I appreciate your help in this matter.

Sincerely,

[Your Name]

You can use one letter to list all accounts that need to be updated at each credit bureau. Most credit bureaus now provide easy-to-fill-out forms that accomplish the same thing. Use these "Request For Reinvestigation" or "Dispute" forms to update your credit report if you can since the credit bureau specifically designed these forms to include all the information you must provide about your accounts.

Of course, I still encourage you to include a nice, short note — even a handwritten one — along with your form. A pleasant letter often makes for speedier results.

Two other common post-bankruptcy credit report errors you should look for are:

• A collection agency listed separately from the creditor it serves. Why should you look like you have two debts when you only have one? Since the debt was discharged under your bankruptcy, only the original creditor should be listed.

• Closed accounts that are listed as open — or as being closed by a creditor (make sure they're listed as being closed by *you* if you are the one who closed them). One exception: if a creditor lists a closed account as open, and the payment history is all positive, leave that account alone, since it shows your past payment history in the best light possible.

Remember to update all incorrect information at each and every credit bureau. You never know which credit bureau a creditor will use to check your credit — and I don't want you to be turned down for credit in the future when the negative information you cleared up on *one* credit report shows up again unexpectedly on another credit bureau's credit report.

Finally, looking at your credit report, you need to check for incorrect information on existing debts. When I applied for a car loan, I was up-front with the loan officer about my past bankruptcy. Everything was going smoothly until the loan officer got my credit report, which showed an unpaid lien from a landlord I'd had — five years before. Since I had no idea there was a judgment against me, I also had no idea the judgment was on my credit report.

I had to call the landlord's attorney to find out how much I owed ($93). Then I had to go in person to pay the money and get a receipt. Then I had to take the receipt to the courthouse to prove the lien had been satisfied. The courthouse gave me a certificate of release. Finally, I got my car loan. I could have easily avoided all that running around and solved everything through the mail if I had known what was on my credit report *before* I applied for my car loan.

Bringing Your Credit Reports Up-To-Date

Just because an overdue bill has been paid, however, doesn't mean that all negative information about the account will be erased from your credit report. Errors show up all the time. Luckily, it's easy for you to get out-of-date and incorrect information removed from your credit report.

Let's say you find incorrect information in your credit report regarding a debt for which you have a bad payment history. You need to make sure that even the negative information is being reported correctly, so it reflects your credit history in the best possible light.

You may have existing debts that weren't included in your bankruptcy. Perhaps you have a personal reason for not including a particular debt (maybe it's a loan you had someone co-sign for).

Or maybe the debt couldn't be discharged under your bankruptcy, which might be the case for a defaulted student loan or back taxes, or the remaining payments on your mortgage once your Chapter 13 repayment plan ended. Anytime you have existing debts that have a bad payment history, I urge you to pay close attention to them. You can bet future creditors will! Start by making sure that the information listed in your credit report is accurate.

If a creditor shows you were 60 days late on several payments, while your checks or receipts prove you were only 30 days late, write the credit bureau and let them know they've got the wrong information. To a creditor, there's a big difference between being 60 days late and being 30 days late.

Find the "Request For Reinvestigation" or "Dispute" form that the credit bureau included with your credit report. Fill out the form, listing which information is wrong, and what the correct information should be. If you don't have this form, simply write a letter to the credit bureau requesting an investigation of the information you believe to be incorrect. Here's a very effective letter you can use.

(Date)

[Credit Bureau]
[Address]
[City, State, Zip]
Re: [Your Social Security Number and/or Account Number]

Dear Sir/Madam:

My credit report shows that [Name of creditor] lists my account as having been delinquent ____ days, _____ times.

I believe this is an error. Please ask this creditor to provide proof of these delinquent payments. If no such proof is found within [30 days in most states; 10 in Maine; 45 in Louisiana], please update my file and remove this information, as required by law.

I thank you in advance for your help in this matter.

Sincerely,

[Your Name]

Start a file for each credit bureau and keep a copy of all letters — and forms — that you send. And remember to always send your letters via certified mail, return receipt requested so that you have proof of the date when you sent your request.

The credit bureau will then contact your creditor to be sure that the information is correct. If the creditor cannot verify the incorrect information, by law, the credit bureau must drop it from your report.

You can expect to hear from the credit bureau in about 45 days. If a month and a half goes by and you still haven't heard anything, write another letter requesting an update on your investigation. Again, send the letter via certified mail, return receipt requested, and keep a copy of your letter.

If you still don't get a response, contact the Federal Trade Commission (FTC). For the number of the nearest FTC office, call 800/688-9889. The FTC regulates credit bureaus and will help you work through any problems you encounter.

Don't volunteer copies of any receipts or canceled checks unless the creditor claims the information is correct. Any creditor who can't back up their claims must remove *all* the bad information — even if you really were late paying!

Without proof, your creditor must upgrade your account to show that you weren't delinquent at all — even if you had been 30 days late in the past.

You could actually wind up with positive credit information on your credit report, if the creditor shows that you've always been current in your payments. In the very worst case, your records would show you were 30 days — rather than 60 days — late (still a big improvement).

Take me, for instance. I had defaulted on my student loan when I was a struggling writer living in New York. Which means my account was at least 120 days past due for quite a while. After declaring bankruptcy, I worked out a payment schedule with the student loan issuer — but, thanks to a computer glitch, my account fell further and further behind.

Every few months I called the creditor who assured me by phone and letter that everything was fine and that my account was current. But they never notified the credit bureau. When I applied for a car loan, the banker was ready to turn down my loan based on the information in my credit report.

When I finally requested my credit report, I saw what my creditors had been seeing: a really bad post-bankruptcy debt — even though I had been diligently making payments on this debt after declaring bankruptcy.

I sent a letter to the credit bureau questioning the creditor's payment history. The credit bureau investigated and responded with a letter stating that the creditor had confirmed that the information was correct!

Once I stopped storming around the house, I called the creditor myself. I calmly explained the problem and asked for a letter stating that my account was — and had been — current, and that the problem was a computer error.

With this letter in hand, I went back to my banker and I was able to get my car loan. More importantly, I sent a copy of this letter to the credit bureau as proof that the account was current — and they updated the account to show that it was never delinquent.

If you have an error on your credit report and the credit bureau says your creditor claims the incorrect information is correct, call or write to your creditor directly and ask them for a letter stating that the account is current (or the correct status).

Once you receive a letter from your creditor saying your account is current, make copies and send one copy to each credit bureau that is reporting the wrong information about your account, along with the following letter.

(Date)

[Credit Bureau]
[Address]
[City, State, Zip]
Re: [Your Social Security Number and Account Number]

Dear Sir/Madam:

My credit report shows that [name of creditor] lists my account as having been delinquent _____ days, _____ times.

You investigated this matter for me on [date they sent you notice that information had been confirmed] and were notified by the creditor that the account was correct as reported.

Enclosed is a letter from the above creditor, showing the correct current status of this account.

Please update my file to show the correct status and remove the negative information from my credit report, as required by law, within the next [30 days in most states; 10 in Maine; 45 in Louisiana].

I thank you in advance for your help in this matter. Please send me a revised copy of my credit report with the new updated information.

Sincerely,

[Your Name]

What If You Run Into A Snag

The credit bureaus should respond about 30 days after receiving your letter. (Maine must respond in 10 days; Louisiana has up to 45 days.) If you have trouble with a credit bureau and they refuse to remove incorrect or out-of-date information from your credit report, write to the Federal Trade Commission (FTC).

In your letter, include the name of the credit bureau, its address and phone number. Explain your problem, the dates you contacted the credit bureau, and with whom you spoke. Include copies of any documents pertaining to your problem. Then send a copy of the whole packet — including your letter and a copy of your documentation — to the credit bureau. Your letter should get someone at the credit bureau to sit up and take notice of your problem. And it'll make the FTC step in. Here's an example of an effective complaint letter which you can send to the FTC:

(Date)

Federal Trade Commission
6th & Pennsylvania Avenue, NW
Washington, DC 20580
Re: [Your Social Security Number and Account Number]

Dear Sir/Madam:

On (Date), I requested a copy of my credit report from [credit bureau name]. On (Date), I sent a letter requesting that the following information be updated: [Account name and number. Explain why information is incorrect or out-of-date.]. To date, [name of credit bureau] has failed to update the following information on my credit report, even though I provided documentation.

Enclosed is a copy of the [type of documentation] already submitted to [name of credit bureau], proving that the information on my credit report is incorrect. I thank you in advance for your help in this matter.

Sincerely,
[Your Name]

cc: [Credit Bureau Name]

You can also complain to your State Attorney General's Office, or Office of Consumer Protection. You'll find these offices listed in the blue pages of your telephone book.

Sometimes, you may run into a snag where a tax lien still shows that you owe money even if you paid it off under your Chapter 13 bankruptcy agreement. If the credit bureaus still show the tax lien is unpaid, write down the names and addresses of all the courthouses where the lien was filed. You'll find this information on your credit reports, listed with the tax lien. Once you have this information in hand, call the IRS at 800/829-1040 and ask them to send a release to all the courthouses.

The sooner you start correcting the errors on your credit report, the better. Begin cleaning up your credit report today. The process may take a few months, but it's definitely worth the trouble. Remember: The sooner you update your credit report, the sooner your credit improves.

Writing a Statement About Your Credit History

The Fair Credit Reporting Act (FCRA) allows you to add a statement to your credit report, explaining any outside factors that led to you declaring bankruptcy. This statement becomes a permanent part of your credit report until you change it. Bankruptcy is often caused by outside factors such as a job loss, illness, divorce — in my case, excessive drinking — that may now be under control. Use your statement to summarize the nature of your past problem and, if possible, show creditors how you are better able to handle credit now.

If the credit bureau limits your statement to fewer than 100 words, the bureau must help you prepare a summary. Call and ask the credit bureau for help writing your statement. Their representatives can help you put your past credit history in the best light. Adding a statement about why you declared bankruptcy, and what you've changed to prevent it from happening again, is one of the best ways to improve your credit report.

Cleaning up your credit report is just the first step. To rebuild your credit, you also need to keep up with your future credit payments at all times. Know all the due dates for your bills, and make sure you put your payments in the mail early enough so that they never arrive late.

Credit Repair Warning Signs

Updating your credit report will take a little time and energy on your part, but it is worth it. It might seem like updating your credit report would be a lot easier if you could just pay someone else to take care of it for you, right? Don't do it!

Most credit repair companies are scams. The simple truth is, no one can get *true* negative information off your credit report for good. Correct information — good and bad — stays on your record for seven years. Your bankruptcy will stay on your report for ten years (and no more than seven years after you finish repaying your debts under Chapter 13 bankruptcy). There is no legitimate way to remove a bankruptcy from your credit report.

But that doesn't mean that you've got a "black mark" on your credit report. It simply means that the credit bureaus will report that you had a bankruptcy in the past. It's up to *you* to take the steps necessary to turn that bankruptcy into an asset. And I know you can do it!

As you've just seen, you can build up your credit rating by improving or updating the existing negative information so it reflects you in the best light. You're better off doing this yourself than you are paying someone to do it for you. All it takes is five to six hours of your time. When you're done, you'll know that your credit report contains the best possible credit history it can. And you'll know you didn't get ripped off by a credit repair scam.

If you did get taken in by a credit repair scam, however, don't beat yourself up. Chalk up the money spent as the fee for an important lesson and move on. Get copies of your current credit reports and start using the information in this chapter to update your credit report yourself.

It's easy to see why many people wind up using credit repair companies. Some companies offer a written guarantee that they'll get negative information off your credit report, or you don't have to pay them. Don't believe it! They'll temporarily give you a clean slate and then they'll take your money (usually $500 to $1,000) and run, before the negative information reappears.

Here are a few Credit Repair Warning Signs that will help keep you from being scammed. Avoid any company that:

1. *Asks for a large up-front fee of several hundred dollars.* Most legitimate companies charge a very small amount for their services, and they don't ask for their money until you are completely satisfied that your credit reports have been corrected.

2. *Says they can remove true, negative information from your credit report.* The methods these companies use can get negative information taken off your credit reports for a short time — but when the creditor reports that the information is correct, it will be back on your reports again. These companies appeal the

bad information on your credit report. By law, the credit bureau must remove the information while it's under investigation. The repair clinic then shows you the next month's credit report, with the negative credit information removed. They charge you their fee, you pay them, and bang — when you apply for a mortgage or a loan down the road — the negative information is back on your credit report and you're out hundreds of dollars.

3. *Assures you that they can remove a bankruptcy from your credit report.* Unless the bankruptcy was discharged over ten years ago (seven years for a Chapter 13), there is no legal way for anyone to remove your bankruptcy. There is a fraudulent way, which involves requesting your bankruptcy file from the courthouse archives, then questioning the listing on your credit report. I don't recommend it.

Having a bankruptcy listed on your report will not prevent you from getting credit. Other negative information can, however, stop you from getting credit you deserve — which is why I encourage you to rebuild your credit history as soon as possible.

If you've been taken advantage of by a credit repair company, contact the Credit Practices Division at the Federal Trade Commission (FTC). To find the number of the nearest FTC office, call 800/688-9889. Once the FTC has a history of consumer complaints against a credit repair company, it can take action to stop the company from continuing business.

One big credit repair company which was sued for credit repair fraud is Credit Resource Management Group (CRMG). Steer clear of these guys.

Finding A Legitimate Credit Repair Company

Legitimate credit repair companies or credit counselors can help you do the perfectly legal strategies that you've just read about. They can write the letters to the creditors on your behalf and work to have negative information updated and have incorrect information removed.

You now have all the tools you need to "do-it-yourself," right here in your hands. But, if you do want to have someone else help you, use the *Credit Repair Warning Signs* I just gave you to make sure the company is on the up and up. I also recommend that you call your State Attorney General's office to find out if the credit repair company is legitimately licensed to do business in your state. You'll find your State Attorney General's office listed in the blue pages of your telephone book.

If you know where the company is headquartered, you can check with the Better Business Bureau in that state to see if the company has any complaints on file. If the company isn't licensed to do business in your state, or has a long record of complaints about it, keep your money in your pocket.

What To Do While You're Waiting For Your Credit Report

You'll have a few weeks to wait for your credit reports — so put this time to good use. Dive into Chapter 2, where you'll find easy-to-use strategies for getting rid of your remaining debt.

If compulsive spending has been a problem for you in the past (wanting to live beyond your means and using credit cards or other forms of debt to accomplish this desire), then you might want to turn to Chapter 10 for some useful information on breaking free from your debt addiction.

Chapter 1: Action Items

1. Order copies of your credit reports from the three major credit bureaus so you know what creditors are seeing about your credit history.

2. Start files for your credit reports and keep copies of all correspondence and conversations you have with creditors or the credit bureaus.

3. Check your personal information on all reports, check for out-of-date information and update all accounts discharged in your bankruptcy.

4. Look for other common post-bankruptcy errors — including debts that are listed more than once and closed accounts that are still listed as open.

5. Bring all negative information up-to-date.

6. Follow-up if a credit bureau doesn't correct a problem. Go straight to the creditor to get the information you need to update your credit report, if necessary.

7. Write a statement about your credit history to explain what caused your bankruptcy.

8. If you're approached by a credit repair company, use the *Credit Repair Warning Signs* as a guideline to make sure they're legitimate — and call your State Attorney General's office to see if the company is licensed to do business in your state.

chapter 2

Getting Rid of Your Remaining Debts

Chances are, before you declared bankruptcy you were making minimum payments on a number of debts. If you've recently declared bankruptcy, and you're waiting for your bankruptcy to be discharged, use the money that you once put toward these bills to prepay for household items instead. Stock up on essential items, buy new shoes for the kids or prepay the utilities.

Once your debts are discharged — whether through Chapter 7 or Chapter 13 — use my *Debt-Buster Strategy* to easily deal with your remaining debts so you can start improving your credit today. To create your *Debt-Buster Strategy*, first add up how much you were paying on your debts before your bankruptcy.

Now that you no longer have to pay these debts, you can write a check to yourself for half that amount — or even one-tenth of that amount — and send it directly to your savings account. If you don't already have a savings account, put down this book right now, go to your bank and open a savings account! You won't ever miss the money if you start setting it aside now.

Each month, write yourself a check and deposit it into your savings account. It's okay to start small, but I strongly suggest that you make your check out for at least $25 every month, so you can quickly see your account balance grow. Deposit just $25 a month and within four months you'll have saved $100.

If the temptation to take the money out of your savings account is too great, visit your bank teller and ask to buy U.S. Savings Bonds. You can buy these bonds for as little as $25 each (for a $50 bond). Most banks will set up an automatic plan for you, buying your bonds automatically each month by taking money out of your checking account. Many employers will do the same, or will let you put your money into a credit union savings account, directly from your paycheck. Just make sure you don't have an ATM card on this account. This way, you won't be tempted to withdraw the money every time you visit your bank.

For now, no matter what comes your way, don't touch this money. Keep letting it grow. When it reaches $500, congratulate yourself. At just $25/month, you can save $500 in under two years. At $50 a month, you can save $500 in just 10 months. That $500 of savings will come in handy when you're working to rebuild your credit.

Why should you set this money aside? Because you'll need it to apply for a secured credit card — the next step in restoring your credit history (see Chapter 4). This savings account will also protect you if an emergency pops up while you're paying down your bills. Once you have your secured credit card, pay off your credit card bill each month.

What If a Creditor Tries to Collect a Discharged Debt?

Be on the lookout for any letters from creditors whose debts were discharged under your bankruptcy. Sometimes, computer-generated letters cross in the mail with the discharge papers, and you can clear up the misunderstanding with a single phone call. Other times, however, a creditor may attempt to collect on a discharged debt or repossess merchandise that they gave up any security interest in.

Any attempt to collect on a discharged debt, or to repossess merchandise more than 60 days after your discharge date — if the creditor didn't contact you in an attempt to have you reaffirm the debt — violates the Bankruptcy Protection Act. If a creditor attempts to collect a discharged debt, send this letter:

(Date)

[Creditor's Name]
[Address]
[City, State, Zip]
Re: [Your Social Security Number and Account Number]

Dear Sir/Madam:

On [date], I received a [letter, or phone call] from you attempting to collect on the above referenced debt.

On [date of discharge], this account was discharged under bankruptcy, [bankruptcy case number]. I trust that you will update your records to show that this debt has been discharged under bankruptcy and is no longer an outstanding debt. I also trust you will notify all credit bureaus that this debt was discharged under bankruptcy.

Enclosed is a copy of my final discharge paper and a copy of my bankruptcy schedule showing your debt listed. As you know, any attempt to collect on a discharged debt is in violation of both the Fair Debt Collection Act and the Bankruptcy Protection Law.

Any further contact from you regarding collection of this debt will be brought to the attention of the bankruptcy court as evidence of your violation and I will exercise my right to bring suit against you and recover damages of $1,000 or more for each incident, as is my right. I thank you in advance for your help in clearing up this matter and I trust that you will not attempt to collect this debt again.

Sincerely,

[Your Name]

cc: Federal Trade Commission
6th & Pennsylvania Avenue, NW
Washington, DC 20580

What to Do About Bounced Checks

If you bounced checks before your bankruptcy, there's a very good chance that you'll run into some difficulty trying to open up a new checking account. That's because banks subscribe to special services like TeleCheck which help them screen new accounts. Any checks you might have bounced should have been included in your bankruptcy. And they should be reported to TeleCheck as being discharged under bankruptcy.

If you apply for a checking account and are turned down, ask the banker for the name and number of the screening service they used. You may get this information automatically, in a letter from the banker, but usually you get turned down in person.

Once you have the name and number of the screening service, call and ask them to send you a listing of checks or accounts that are listed as outstanding. They will tell you the process for clearing your record. Just like when you cleaned up your credit report, you'll need to show the screening service which checks were discharged under bankruptcy. You'll still have to make good on checks that you might have forgotten to include in your bankruptcy, if you want to open up a checking account with that bank.

Do You Pay Income Tax on Discharged Debt?

You do *not* pay income taxes on debts that are discharged under your bankruptcy. Some people get confused about this, so let me set the record straight. If a creditor or a mortgage lender sends you a 1099C and you discharged the debt under your bankruptcy, your creditor has made an honest mistake.

Don't ignore the notice, though, or you'll wind up with a great big IRS headache. To avoid an IRS problem when you file your taxes, attach a copy of the 1099C, a statement that says the debt was discharged under bankruptcy, and a copy of your "Notice of Commencement of Case" and "Order of Discharge" to your tax return.

What To Do With Debts That Weren't Discharged

You'll probably have four different types of debts left if you declared Chapter 7:

1. *Debts you reaffirmed (agreed to keep paying) with a creditor, such as your mortgage or your car loan.*

2. *Debts to friends or relatives you decided to repay.*

3. *Student loans.* You may need to petition the bankruptcy court to confirm that your student loans were actually discharged. This happened to me. My student loan had not been in repayment for seven years from the date the first payment became due, because of the deferments I had taken. Therefore, my student loans weren't dischargeable, even though they were listed in my bankruptcy. So, even though your student loans are listed on your bankruptcy papers, they may not be discharged if they don't qualify to be discharged.

Student loans are currently dischargeable only if they've been in repayment for at least seven years from the date the first payment became due, but the clock stops any time you enter deferment or get a forbearance on the loan. There's a slim chance that Congress will change the laws, so ask your attorney whether or not your student loan should have been dischargeable.

4. *Taxes that weren't discharged under your Chapter 7 bankruptcy.* In most cases, taxes that were filed on time at least two years prior to your bankruptcy can be included in your bankruptcy. Otherwise you'll have to repay them afterwards.

In addition, if you declared Chapter 13 bankruptcy, you may still owe on your student loans, alimony or child support, or back taxes. If you still owe back taxes, talk with your accountant about getting an *Offer In Compromise* from the IRS so you can continue making payments under a repayment plan.

We'll talk about how to pay off your larger debts like your car loan and mortgage when we get to Chapter 5 and Chapter 9. For now, we're going to concentrate on eliminating any other remaining debts as quickly as possible. So...now that you're putting a portion of the money you were spending on bills into a savings account, what should you do with the rest of the money? Pay off your remaining bills.

Don't just apply your extra cash haphazardly toward one bill or another. Instead, use the following *DebtBuster Strategy* and you'll not only eliminate your debts quicker — you'll also pay less interest! Lay out all your remaining debts on the table and I'll show you how to bounce back from bankruptcy.

Putting The DebtBuster Strategy To Work For You

You'll find a sample *DebtBuster Strategy Sheet* on page 67. Feel free to make a copy of this page to use as a worksheet. On your *DebtBuster Strategy Sheet*, list of all your outstanding debts, their balances, and the interest rates they charge under Columns A, B and C. Divide the amount you owe on that bill by

12. Write down that amount on your list under Column D. Next, write down the amount of your monthly finance charge under Column E. Add your principal payment (D) and your monthly finance charge (E) together and enter this amount in Column F. This is the amount you need to pay every month *if you want to pay off that debt in full in one year*.

For example, say your balance on your first debt is $1,200. Divided by 12, your principal payment would be $100. If you're paying 20% interest, you're paying a $20 finance charge every month. Your combined monthly payment (principal and finance charge) would be $120 if you want to pay off your card in one year.

Need More Time To Pay Down Your Debts?

Don't worry if you can't pay these amounts all at once. You may have more debt left after your bankruptcy than can reasonably be paid off in one year. That's okay. This is where the last column of the ***DebtBuster Strategy*** comes into play. You can start to pay down your balances faster by paying the minimum monthly payments listed on your bills *plus the interest that was added to this month's bill*. Add these amounts and enter the total in Column G.

For example, let's say that your minimum monthly payment is $30, and your interest payment is $20. If you can, pay $50 this month — the $30 minimum plus the $20 interest that accrued. If you do, your entire minimum monthly payment is *principal* because you've paid the interest separately. And next month, your balance will actually be $30 lower — instead of just $10 lower! Remember to pay that same amount each month — $50 in this example — even if the creditor lowers your minimum payment. Creditors lower your minimum payment so they can keep getting you to pay them more interest.

Still too much to pay? Start smaller, then, by just paying the minimum monthly payment, which you can enter into Column H. Pay the minimum payments on all your other debts and put all the extra money you can toward paying the debt with the highest interest rate first. For example, if your minimum monthly payment is $80 on the debt with the highest interest rate, then pay $80, plus anything extra you can that month. You'll find solid strategies for "finding" the hidden money in your budget in Chapter 10.

When your first debt is paid off, reward yourself with a gift, then keep paying the same $80 toward your bills. This time, take the $80 you were paying for the now paid-off debt and put it toward the debt with the next highest interest rate. This $80 will be in addition to the minimum payment you're already making on that debt. This will help you pay off your debt faster.

There's a great debate over which debts you should pay off first: the ones with the highest interest rate or the ones with the lowest balance. My recommendation? Use the strategy that suits *you* best.

Paying the Highest Interest Rate Bills First

If you want to reduce the amount of interest that you pay out each month, start by paying off your high-interest-rate cards first. Your department store cards and gas cards are probably the place to start since they generally carry very high interest rates. I looked at the bottom of my Fashion Bug bill one month and noticed that they had listed the "Corresponding Annual Percentage Rate" at 22.9% but also had the "Annual Percentage Rate" listed as

85.8%! When I asked about it, the creditor told me that this was the rate they can charge you when your account becomes delinquent — no wonder people have to declare bankruptcy!

Once you pay your expensive department store and gas card bills, you'll free up even more cash to pay your other bills. Pay the minimum payment on your other bills (or $5-$10 on bills with no minimum payment) each month. Paying off the bill with the highest interest rate will save you the most money in the long run, which is why it's the method I recommend using.

Paying the Smallest Balance Bills First

Psychologically, however, you may *feel better* if you pay off your bills with the smallest balances first. Some people like to see physical proof of their progress — which you certainly get when you can hold up a bill and say "another one paid in full!" If this is the case for you, pick the bill with the smallest balance and pay that one off first. If you have several bills with the same small balance due, pay the small bill with the highest interest rate first.

Once you pay off a bill, keep using that money to pay down your other bills. Add the amount you had been paying on that bill to the amount you send to one of your remaining creditors, preferably the creditor with the next highest interest rate. For example, if you pay $35 a month on your dentist's bill, once it's paid off you can start paying an extra $35 on your student loan. This causes a waterfall effect, helping you pay off your other bills even quicker. Within a year, chances are very good that you'll be well on your way to a debt-free life, and back on track again. This only works, however, if you cut up your credit cards or stick them in the deep freeze. You can't get out of debt if you're adding more debt to the load.

Look at the *DebtBuster Strategy Sheet* on page 67 for a minute. As you can see, one way to keep track of the amount you're paying toward your debts is to write that amount in the bottom column of the table. *Try to always pay at least that total amount toward your debts each month, no matter what.*

Resist the temptation to spend the "extra, found money" on new stuff until your old debts are paid off. You don't have to deny yourself completely, though. You might want to reward yourself the month after you pay off one debt by getting something special for yourself that costs half of what you were paying on that bill each month. This way, every time you retire another debt, you get to gift yourself with something of increasing value. Even better, brainstorm and find a free way to reward yourself.

There's another reason it's important to keep track of how much you originally spend each month toward your debts. As your balances drop credit card companies reduce your required minimum payments. Don't veer from your strategy. Continue to pay at least the amount that is listed in the bottom column of your *DebtBuster Strategy Sheet* to make sure that you continue to pay down your debts as quickly as possible. The faster you pay off these debts, the faster you'll break the debt cycle — for good!

If you're currently behind on any of your debts, start by putting every extra penny toward getting the past due bills caught up, before paying anything toward the interest.

If you want to set up your *DebtBuster Strategy* on the computer, I recommend using *Quicken, Excel* or another spreadsheet type program like *No Bills!*. List your credit cards one by one on the computer, with the highest interest rate debt at the top and the lowest interest rate debts at the bottom. This way you always know which debt should get any extra money each month.

Once you pay off the highest interest rate debt, delete it, and start paying more toward the next highest interest rate debt that is still on the list.

I know there will be times when you'll really want to buy something. And you can buy these items — using the savings that you've started to build up. Make a commitment to yourself not to use credit right now. Instead, get used to creating new, healthier "money habits." I guarantee that if you put off your purchases for one year and follow the *DebtBuster Strategy*, you'll find yourself in great shape financially, building up your savings, out of debt, and able to pay *cash* for everything you want to buy.

You might also want to consider using a service such as *All Paid* from MyVesta.org (formerly Debt Counselors of America; 800/680-3328), which lets you pay off your debt with one simple monthly payment — without having to take out a loan. MyVesta personally tailors each *All Paid* program to help you accelerate the repayment of your remaining debts.

You tell MyVesta what amount you'd like to pay each month toward your debts. Then you photocopy all the bills you want to include and highlight the current balance on the debt, the minimum monthly payment due on the debt, the address where payments should be sent and the current interest rate charged on that debt. When you have everything together, and a copy of their Assistance Agreement, send it all to MyVesta.org at 6 Taft Court, Suite 200, Rockville, MD 20850.

MyVesta then calculates the best way to pay your debts so that you save the most interest. And you don't have to worry about writing out different checks for each creditor — your future bills are sent directly to MyVesta, you write one check to MyVesta each month and they take care of paying the bills for you. To learn more about the program, you can call MyVesta at the number above, or check out their website at http://www.myvesta.org.

Using Your Computer For Debt Repayment

You may prefer to use your computer to set up and track your debt repayment. If so, you might want to check out these few programs:

1. *Quicken 6.0 Deluxe*; $54.99. This version contains an excellent debt repayment feature. You can fool around with the "what if" scenarios until the cows come home.

2. *No Bills! Credit Card Eliminator*; $30. (CFinders Software, P.O. Box 372103, Satellite Beach, FL 32937; 800/599-3783; 407/255-2151). This shareware will tell you how long it will take you to pay off your debts based on minimum payments, annual percentage rates (APRs), etc.

You can download *No Bills!* for free if you have **America On-Line**. Go to "Keyword: Shareware" and then do a search for Applications called "NO BILLS." You can download and use the trial version of *No Bills!* for 21 days with no charge. If you want to keep using the program, you can purchase a registered copy for $30. For more details, check out http://www.cfinders.com.

Repaying Your Student Loans

Chances are, your student loans probably weren't discharged under your bankruptcy.

If you declared Chapter 7, or if you still owe money on student loans that you were repaying under a Chapter 13 bankruptcy, you'll have to work out a repayment schedule. Once you make your final payment under a Chapter 13 bankruptcy, your student loan lender will take over payments from you.

When you're approached with a payment schedule, offer to pay half of what they say you must pay each month — and work your way up to a monthly payment you can afford.

If you have defaulted on your student loans, and they weren't discharged under your bankruptcy (remember, just because you listed them on your bankruptcy schedule doesn't make them dischargeable!), there's nothing you need to do right now. You'll soon hear from your lender requesting repayment of the student loan. Don't panic if they demand payment in full or a monthly amount that is more than you can afford. Write a letter to the lender and tell them *exactly* how much you can afford to pay each month. Here's a sample letter that you can use:

(Date)

[Student Loan Lender]
[Address]
[City, State, Zip]
Re: [Your Social Security number and/or loan number]

Dear Sir/Madam:

I have recently discovered that the above-referenced loan was not discharged under my bankruptcy dated [date of your discharge].

At this time, I am able to pay [amount per month you KNOW you can pay each month] per month toward this debt. I would like to work out a repayment plan with you directly so that I can get this loan paid off.

Please let me know if this payment amount is satisfactory and send me a repayment booklet so I can begin repaying this loan.

As an act of good faith, I have enclosed a check in the amount of [amount per month you KNOW you can pay each month], as my first payment on this loan. I appreciate your help in getting this loan repaid.

Sincerely,

[Your name]

Remember: Your student loan lender wants their money any way they can get it. They will happily set up a repayment plan that will work for you.

Consolidating Your Student Loans

Another way to bring your student loans up-to-date is to consolidate them under one of the federal student loan consolidation programs. If you've defaulted on your student loans, and the Department of Education holds your loans, call 800/621-3115 to see what your options might be for consolidation. This isn't the most friendly automated system (the computer voice needs customer service school!), but you will eventually get your questions answered if you provide the information requested.

There are two federal programs that can help you consolidate your loans — the Loan Consolidation Center which handles the *William D. Ford Federal Direct Consolidation Loan Program* (800/557-7392) and the Network Consolidation Center which handles the *Sallie Mae Loan Consolidation Program* (800/338-5000). Once you consolidate your loans, you can never again defer them. So, if you're thinking of going back to school anytime soon, you may not want to consolidate your student loans.

Chances are good that you can get a lower interest rate from these consolidation programs than you're paying now. However, if the interest rate is higher on any of your current student loans, you can choose not to consolidate that loan, so you don't wind up paying extra interest.

The interest rate on the Ford consolidation program is capped and can only be adjusted annually. The variable rate they charge can never exceed 8.25% if you took out the loan, or 9% if you're a parent and the loan is a PLUS loan.

If you're interested in consolidating your student loans, call these organizations and request information from them and find out which of your loans qualify for which program. They'll each send you a brochure explaining their programs. The Ford program offers four different repayment options.

1. *Income Contingent Repayment Plan.* If you borrowed the money as a student, you can use this option, where your monthly payment is based on your annual income and the loan amount. Your payments go up or down with your income, and you have up to 25 years to repay your loans. After 25 years, any balance is forgiven, although it may be taxable.

2. *Standard Repayment Plan.* Under this plan you'll pay at least $50 a month for up to 10 years. Note that the key phrase here is "up to" — there's no guarantee that you'll get the whole 10 years to repay your loan. Ford calculates your actual payment amount and repayment plan according to your loan amount, so you may need to go back and forth with them several times to get a payment you can actually afford.

3. *Extended Repayment Plan.* This plan gives you 12-30 years to repay your student loans, which is the repayment plan I would recommend. You'll pay at least $50 a month, but your payment will definitely be less than it would be under the Standard Repayment Plan. You can always pay extra each month, when you have extra cash. This will help you save on the interest that you'll be paying over the years.

4. *Graduated Repayment Plan.* Like the Extended Repayment Plan, this plan gives you 12-30 years to repay your loan. However your payment starts out low and gradually increases every two years. Since there's no guarantee that your income will

continue to increase gradually, I'd recommend going with the Extended Repayment Plan instead.

When you get the brochure from the student loan consolidator, fill out the coupon to request an application and an estimate of how much your monthly payment might be under their program. They'll do the calculations and send you an estimate of what your payments would be under each repayment plan. If you're approved, you would then have only one payment to make each month, for all the student loans you consolidated.

To Reaffirm or Not To Reaffirm

I know firsthand how difficult it can be to decide whether or not you should keep paying on items that you bought before your bankruptcy. Especially if it's an item that has special value to you. If you decide to keep the item, you and your creditor enter into a signed agreement known as a "Reaffirmation Agreement."

You agree to continue to be responsible for the debt, and they agree to let you keep your property, or the credit card. In most cases, you have to continue paying on the debt if you want to keep the item. If you are able to stay current with your reaffirmed debts, and pay them off completely, your reaffirmed debts will show up as excellent post-bankruptcy credit references. Future creditors look very favorably on these reaffirmed accounts — if you're able to pay them off.

Creditors will care more about your most recent 1-2 year payment history than they will about your past payment history or your bankruptcy. If you're worried that money might be tight, then you might be better off not reaffirming any unsecured debts. You can rebuild your credit history better with a fresh start than if you're trying to tread water paying off a debt that could have been discharged under your bankruptcy.

Over the years, as the Bankruptcy Guru on **America On-Line's** *Moneywhiz* personal finance forum (now *theWhiz.com*), I've listened to many people agonize over whether or not they should keep, or "reaffirm" debts that range from computer equipment and couches to engagement rings and cars. You may have agonized over decisions for similar items you bought before your bankruptcy.

You're not alone. Many of us confuse our self-worth with our "stuff" or we have a lot of emotional attachment to items that mark rites of passages in our lives. You may be worried about *"what will the neighbors think if they see our furniture is missing?"* Or you may be very attached to your car, especially if it's the first new car you've ever owned. These are all perfectly natural feelings to have. But you may need to make some hard decisions now about whether or not continuing to pay for these items is the best thing for you financially at this point. To make this decision easier on you, I've included my rule of thumb for reaffirming debts. You're usually better off reaffirming a debt, *only* if an item meets these two criteria:

1. *The item should be a necessity for daily living such as a vehicle or household appliance.*

2. *The creditor must be willing to reaffirm for no more than the actual* <u>value</u> *of the item, which may be considerably less than the amount you still owe on the debt.*

You'll always be better off discharging every debt you can. Then you can start to rebuild your finances and replace items one at a time, buying them with *cash*. If you only reaffirm *necessary items*, you'll soon find that you actually have enough cash to replace the items you gave up.

If you do decide to reaffirm debts for other items, such as for a computer, or a TV, don't reaffirm the debt when you file your initial bankruptcy paperwork. Instead, wait to see if the creditor shows up or if the debt gets discharged under the bankruptcy. In most states, unless your creditor shows up at your creditors' hearing or places their claim on the item within 60 days of your discharge date, the debt will be discharged and the merchandise is yours. In others, you'll need to sign a statement saying that you've reaffirmed, redeemed or surrendered the item.

If a creditor shows up at your creditors' hearing, or places a claim on the merchandise, they'll usually ask you to reaffirm the debt or surrender the merchandise. But you actually have a third option, which is to pay the value of the merchandise (usually less than the amount of the debt).

If you stick to your guns and tell the creditor that they can have the merchandise back, chances are that the creditor will back down and offer you a lower balance on the debt in order to get some money back. At that point, it will be up to you to decide whether you want to keep the item and pay the creditor a smaller amount of money, or turn over the item. I recommend *against* reaffirming secured debts unless the law says you must. Redeeming the item, is a better strategy.

For example, one woman had bought a $300 television from Sears. At her creditors' meeting, a Sears representative showed up and said, *"Reaffirm or we'll repossess the TV."* She said, *"Okay, repossess it."* That wasn't what Sears wanted to hear. So the Sears representative said again, *"No, you don't understand — you need to reaffirm or we'll repossess."* She said, *"Well, it's worth $150* *to me, take it or leave it."* Sears took the $150, she kept her television, and everybody was happy.

What To Do If You've Already Reaffirmed Other Debts

As my friend Ken Dolan likes to say, "shoulda, woulda, coulda" — if you reaffirmed other debts, what's done is done and there's no reason to beat yourself up having reaffirmed debts you might have been better off letting go. You may still have a few options available which you can use, especially if money is still tight after your bankruptcy is discharged.

If your bankruptcy was discharged less than 60 days ago, surrendering the item would probably be your best option. One woman discovered that after declaring bankruptcy her family budget was still "upside down," with more money going out than was coming in. After looking over their budget, they discovered that if they surrendered one of the cars which had a reaffirmed loan, their budget would even itself out.

Surrendering an item within 60 days of your bankruptcy is a pretty easy action to take. Call your bankruptcy attorney, or the trustee or clerk for the bankruptcy court where you had your creditors' hearing and tell them that you want to surrender an item that was reaffirmed under your bankruptcy, because you've realized that you really can't afford to keep that debt. You'll need to resubmit your revised "Intention To Reaffirm" paperwork, which will cost you about $20.

Once you submit the revised "Intention To Reaffirm" to the court, call your lender and arrange a time to have the item picked up. Be sure to get a signed and dated receipt when you turn over the item you're surrendering. Read the papers carefully and do not sign any agreement that would make you responsible for any future debt on this item.

Even if you declared bankruptcy *years* ago, you may still be able to get out from under a reaffirmation agreement that you're paying on. Any time you sign a reaffirmation agreement with a creditor, the creditor must — by law — file their reaffirmation papers with the court.

The bankruptcy judge then reviews your case and determines whether or not you can reasonably be expected to pay the reaffirmed debt, based on your current financial situation. Some creditors, however, don't file their reaffirmation agreements with the court.

Either they can't be bothered to take the time, or they know that you probably can't afford to keep up with the payments. In that case, they are attempting to get you to pay a debt that should have been discharged under your bankruptcy. And they use your emotional attachment to the item to pressure you into paying for an item that is worth far less than what you owe.

What to Do If A Creditor Didn't
File Your Reaffirmation Agreement

Sears practiced this particular brand of pressure tactics for years in order to get consumers to reaffirm their Sears credit card accounts. In 1997, Sears lost a class action lawsuit and signed an agreement to repay bankrupt Americans who were pressured into reaffirming and repaying debts that were actually discharged under their bankruptcies, between 1985 and 1997.

Under the settlement terms of the class action lawsuit, Sears had to repay $100 million dollars' worth of principal and interest that was paid to them by 200,000 consumers under reaffirmation agreements which either weren't properly filed or weren't approved by the bankruptcy judges.

If you filed a Chapter 7 bankruptcy between 1985 and 1997 and either Sears or Western Auto Supply Company (a subsidiary of Sears) was listed as a creditor and they pressured you into repaying your debt under threat of losing the merchandise you had in your possession, you would have been eligible to a refund of all the money you paid, plus interest. In addition, Sears sent out $100 gift certificates as a gesture of goodwill to everyone involved.

If a creditor didn't properly file your reaffirmation agreement, you can petition the court to have the reaffirmation thrown out. Call your attorney or the bankruptcy trustee at your bankruptcy court for details on how to handle your specific case.

If the reaffirmation agreement is thrown out, the judge will decide whether or not you can keep the reaffirmed items or receive a refund for the payments you've made so far. In some cases, people have been able to keep the reaffirmed item *and* receive a refund for the money they've already paid.

When Does It Pay to Reaffirm a Credit Card

You may be tempted to give yourself a "leg up" after bankruptcy by reaffirming debt on a credit card. For department store cards, like those issued by Sears or Montgomery Wards, the items are secured by a "security interest clause" in the small print on the credit card application. By reaffirming the debt, you're agreeing to pay the balance due on the secured item. This may or may not be a good move, and you should again use my two guidelines above to decide if reaffirming is right for you.

But what about a VISA or MasterCard or American Express card with a low balance remaining? Several things could happen if you pay that balance off before the bankruptcy, or reaffirm the debt through your bankruptcy. I firmly believe that you're always better off letting go of all the credit cards. It's too easy to use them as a crutch to buy things you can't pay cash for right now.

Credit card companies have done an excellent job of convincing us, through their marketing efforts, that we *need to have a credit card*. A good secured credit card will serve you as well as, or even better than, an unsecured card. We'll talk more about secured and unsecured credit cards in Chapter 4. But if you firmly believe that you need an unsecured credit card, you're actually better off reaffirming the debt on a low balance card than you are paying off the balance before you file.

Here's why: If you reaffirm the debt, the creditor knows that you intend to pay off this debt and they have prior knowledge of your bankruptcy. There's one thing to watch out for, however, if you decide to reaffirm a credit card.

Make sure your reaffirmation agreement with the creditor clearly says that your account will remain active, and will be rated as an active account. If the agreement says you'll be "eligible to apply" for credit after the debt is paid off, you're better off *not* reaffirming the debt. In those cases, chances are good that once you pay off the debt the creditor will cancel your credit card.

Reaffirming credit card debt can be expensive *unless* you're actively working to pay off the debt. One man who came to me for help was very frustrated after having reaffirmed a Montgomery Wards credit card. The card had a $500 limit, so he reaffirmed the debt, even though the card was almost completely maxed out.

The minimum payment on his card was $14 a month. The interest rate was 21%. Every month, $8.50 of his $14 payment went to pay off accumulated interest — and $5.50 went toward paying off the $500 balance. At this rate, assuming that he didn't charge anything else to the credit card, it will take him 91 months — over seven and a half years — to pay off that $500 credit card that he could have discharged under his bankruptcy.

The only reason he kept the credit card, was so that he would have a positive credit reference on his credit report. Luckily, he came to me. I recommended that he use the ***DebtBuster Strategy***, and increase his monthly payments to $22.50. This way, he'll pay off his bill in three years instead!

What If You Have a Zero Balance On a Credit Card

You don't have to list credit cards on your bankruptcy schedule if they have no balance due. There's a pretty good chance that you can use this creditor to rebuild your credit history. But there's also a good chance that the creditor will close your account if they discover your bankruptcy. In particular, if you've declared Chapter 13, your creditors may close accounts that you've paid off. To reopen the account, you'll need your trustee's approval to pay that credit card outside your Chapter 13 repayment plan.

One credit bureau, Equifax, now sells a service known as *Navigator*, which provides creditors with the Social Security numbers of anyone who has filed bankruptcy that month. Creditors then compare the list against the Social Security numbers of their cardholders and will often cancel your account without any warning. There's nothing quite as embarrassing as going to buy something with a credit card you didn't include in your bankruptcy, only to discover that the creditor has canceled your card.

Also, some consumers have discovered that their creditors have listed their account as "discharged under bankruptcy" even though it wasn't included in the bankruptcy at all. If this happens to you — especially if you worked hard and spent hundreds or thousands of dollars paying off that debt — there is one strategy that might convince the creditor to reopen your account.

Call the creditor's customer service department and get the phone number for the corporate offices. Then call the corporate offices and get the name and address for the Director of Consumer Affairs. Then send this brief letter, certified, return receipt requested:

(Date)

[Director's Name]
Director of Consumer Affairs
[Address]
[City, State, Zip Code]

Re: [Your account number]

Dear [Director's Name]:

I have been a customer of yours since [date you opened the account with them], with my account in good standing.

While I was forced to declare bankruptcy on [date of bankruptcy discharge], I kept your account out of my bankruptcy because I valued my relationship with you and didn't want to include your company in my bankruptcy.

[Add a paragraph here stating the status of your account with them, such as "my account was closed by your representatives on such-and-such date" or "my account is erroneously listed on my credit report as having been discharged under bankruptcy, but that is not correct."]

Since I've been a customer of yours for [number of years you've been a customer], I would really like to keep this account active and am writing to ask that you reopen this account.

I understand that you may be reluctant to open an account for someone with a recent bankruptcy on their credit report, however, I believe you can minimize your risk if you make my credit limit be [$500 or the current balance on the account, whichever is greater].

I appreciate you taking a chance on a long-time customer who is trying to rebuild [his/her] credit and I trust that you will reinstate my account within the next 30 days.

Sincerely,

[Your name]

This letter lets your creditor see that you're offering good faith, and they aren't taking any undue risk. No matter what decision you made regarding reaffirming a debt, don't beat yourself up. Whatever decision you made was the best decision for you at the time. Now, take whatever steps you can to make sure your reaffirmation is helping you rebuild your credit. Check your credit reports to see how the reaffirmed account is being reported. It should show as being current, if you've made all your payments on time since the bankruptcy.

Falling Behind on Your Reaffirmation Agreement

You're not alone if you had a creditor bully you into signing a reaffirmation agreement, even when you don't think it will be possible for you to make the payments the creditor is asking for. One woman shared her story:

> *We told our attorney that we wanted to reaffirm our two vehicles because we used both of them. We signed the reaffirmation agreements with the banks, even though my husband had no job and I was working but getting ready to go on disability because of my pregnancy.*

Not surprisingly, this woman and her husband fell behind on their reaffirmation agreement. If you find you're having a hard time keeping up with your reaffirmation payments, first see if you can cancel the agreement, or if there's a chance the creditor didn't properly file your reaffirmation papers with the court.

If neither option is available to you, you may have no other choice but to surrender the item you reaffirmed. First, see if the creditor will take the item back in exchange for complete forgiveness of the debt. This is highly unlikely, but it's worth asking. If the creditor won't take the item back, see if you can sell the item and work out a repayment agreement for the balance of the debt. Another way this works is that the creditor might re-possess the item, sell it at auction and charge you the balance of the debt.

Once you've paid off a good chunk of the debt by selling the item you reaffirmed, you may get a little breathing room if you ask the creditor to spread out the remaining balance so your monthly payment is half of what it was under the reaffirmation agreement. Don't worry if the creditor balks, just stick to your guns, let them know this is all you can pay and force them to work with you.

You have the power in this situation, not the creditor. As a general rule, you'll get more money selling the item yourself and applying that money toward paying off the debt.

More than likely, you'll wind up with a small black mark on your credit report if you aren't able to keep up the payments under your reaffirmation agreement. It's not the best thing in the world to have a 30-day or 60-day notation on your credit report *after* your bankruptcy. But it would be worse to have a 120-day notation, or many months of 30-day late pays.

You're far better off cutting your losses, getting rid of the item and working to repay the debt on a schedule you *can* afford, so that you can start getting financially secure again.

Look through the debts you've reaffirmed and see if you should cancel your reaffirmation agreement, return the item, or accelerate repayment with the ***DebtBuster Strategy***. Write down each debt you've reaffirmed and explore your options. You could save yourself hundreds of dollars in interest — and countless hours of lost sleep. Remember: you may not need to reaffirm a secured debt; you may just need to make sure your payments stay current.

As you take each step forward, getting back on your financial feet one step at time, you'll find your cash flow growing month after month. Yes, you will have temporary setbacks every now and then. This is a normal ebb and flow of money. This is why you've started setting aside some savings. Do not despair. Use your savings to even out the ebb and flow. Anytime your financial situation begins to look bleak, remind yourself of your abundance and your prosperity. Sit quietly for twenty minutes and review your finances. As you do so, ask yourself these three questions:

1. *Are you doing everything you can to rebuild your financial future?*

2. *Is there anything you're doing — any place you're spending money — where you can cut back, temporarily, today to get your cash flow back on track?*

3. *What one action can you take today to improve your financial situation?*

The power to change your financial fate is yours — if you choose to use it!

Chapter 2: Action Items

1. Stock up on perishable household goods, buy necessary items you've held off on, or prepay utilities.

2. Start saving some of the money you were paying creditors to build a cash reserve.

3. Create your own personal *DebtBuster Strategy* for your remaining debts so you can start paying them off. Paying the debts off with the highest interest rates first will save you more money in the long run.

4. Double check with the bankruptcy court to see if your student loans were discharged. If you still owe on your student loans, contact one of the federal student loan consolidation programs to work out a repayment plan you can afford.

5. Change any reaffirmation agreements that you can no longer afford. You can either file an amended Intention Statement or appeal to the bankruptcy judge.

6. Speed up repayment of your reaffirmed debts by using the *DebtBuster Strategy*.

*   *   *

All the strategies I've told you about in Chapters 1 and 2 will help you get your credit history into shape — and help you keep it there.

If overspending is a continuing problem for you, I urge you to take a look at the resources in Chapter 10. Your financial well-being is at stake here, so don't be shy about asking for help. I don't want all your hard work so far to be ruined because of old money habits.

Once your credit history is up-to-date, and you're caught up on your bills, it's time to start putting new, positive credit information in front of your old, negative information. Let's get to it — I know you can do it!

DebtBuster Strategy Sheet

	A	B	C	D	E	F	G	H
	Debt Owed To	Balance Remaining	Interest Rate	1/12th Principal	Monthly Interest	Monthly Payment	Req.+ Intrst.	Req. Pymt.
1.	ABC Credit	$1,200.00	20%; $240/yr	$100.00	$20.00	$120.00	$50	$30
2.								
3.								
4.								
5.								
6.								

chapter 3

Breaking the Debt Cycle — For Good!

Once your credit reports are in shape, and you've worked out a strategy to repay your existing debts, you're *almost* ready to start rebuilding your credit. But *first*, you need to make sure you're rebuilding your credit for the right reason.

You're not alone if you view credit as a lifeline to getting access to the things you want in life. But credit can be a heavy anchor of new debt if you're not careful. I started to rebuild my credit with the best intentions — but I found myself with nearly $1,500 in debt on a credit card, five years after my bankruptcy.

Luckily, by studying and researching everything I could about credit, debt and prosperity, I finally became a more credit-savvy consumer. And you can too, if you use the tips in this chapter as guidelines for your financial future.

How To Become a Credit-Savvy Consumer

Being credit-savvy isn't as hard as you might think. There are some simple rules for credit that will help you make the best decisions possible. Knowing this information — and following these rules — will help you be a better credit user:

1. *Check all offers for credit that you receive to see who is the issuing bank.* Real credit cards are issued by banks. All credit card applications must clearly state the name of the issuing bank. Any offers that don't clearly state this information are scams,

which don't offer real credit cards. I fell for one of these scams myself, shortly after I declared bankruptcy.

2. *Always compare the interest rates being charged on different credit cards so you know how much interest you'll be paying.* Store and catalog credit cards have higher interest rates. You'll almost always be better off using a bank credit card (VISA or MasterCard) than a store credit card.

3. *Avoid "Buy Now, Pay Later" offers, which can be very expensive.* Many of us take advantage of "buy now, pay later" offers because we believe we'll have more money coming in when it comes time to pay off the bill. But often, that's not the case. Many of the "buy now, pay later" offers don't charge interest as long as you pay the balance in full before the no-payment period ends. But if you don't pay the bill off in full by that date, you'll wind up being charged all the back interest. It only pays to use these offers if you start making payments right away and pay off the bill in full before the no-payment period ends. This way, you can buy the item over a few months, without paying any interest.

4. *Always read the fine print.* Starting today, take time to read the fine print of any credit applications, as well as any information that alerts you to changes in the way your creditors do business with you. Creditors will often send you statements alerting you to changes in your agreement, which will go into affect if you don't tell them that you object.

This is how creditors "suddenly" raise your interest rate without warning, for example. They do give us warning, but many of us don't ever read the warnings we receive. Whenever you receive something from a creditor, read it carefully. For information you receive for changes to current credit cards or for new credit card applications, always ask yourself three important questions:

• *What interest rate will I be charged?* If the interest rate is too outrageous, call the creditor and complain. If they refuse to lower the interest rate, do yourself a big favor and close the account, pay off the debt and use a credit card from a company that actually values your business.

• *Is there a grace period before the charges I make start accruing interest?* You should have at least 25 days to pay off your bills before you start being charged interest.

• *What other fees and penalties could I be charged?* Know how much you'll have to pay if you go over your credit limit, how much you'll pay if your payment is late or if you bounce a check.

If you're ever not clear on something you read, or have more questions, call the creditor and *ask*. Make sure all your questions are answered *and* you're comfortable before you buy.

5. *Always check to see what the current interest rate is on anything you buy on credit.* The interest rate that is included in the material you receive with new credit card applications is often out of date, usually by a year or more.

Be sure you know what the *current* interest rate is *before* you sign on the dotted line — and beware of teaser rates that jump up after six months. If you can't figure out the current interest rate from the material you've read, call the creditor's customer service representative and ask.

6. *Exercise your right to change your mind about credit purchases.* If you buy a big ticket item on credit (such as

financing new windows), you have three business days in which you can cancel your contract and get any deposit back.

7. *Set aside the money for household credit purchases <u>before</u> you buy.* Of all the ground rules for using credit, this one is probably the hardest one to follow. We've all been in the position where we've had to make an emergency purchase on credit. We've also all been in the position where we've bought something on credit for enjoyment (a vacation, a gift) and we didn't have the money set aside to pay for it.

As a credit-savvy consumer, it's important to remember that you don't want to add new debt to your current expenses. If you want to buy something on credit for enjoyment, find out what it will cost to buy what you want and then set aside the money each month to achieve your goal. If you have an emergency, charge what you need to charge, then don't charge anything else until your balance is paid off.

Stopping any additional credit purchases — no matter how big or small — may seem harsh, but there's a method behind my madness. When I talk with people who are deep in debt, I can easily trace their credit card problems back, using some simple detective work.

Looking at their credit card statements, I can point to the first month they carried a balance after months or years of paying the balance off in full. Usually, some emergency occurred that caused them to buy something they didn't have the money for at the time. Tickets to visit a sick parent, a new household appliance and car repairs top the list. Digging a little deeper, I can look at their statements over a few more months, until the sizable monthly payment they were making suddenly turned into the minimum payments. That's when the second emergency hit; but by then, they had racked up more debt than they could pay off in a few months' time.

8. *Don't believe any sales pitch that says "You have to buy now or you can't get it at this great price."* I grew up surrounded by a family-owned business and I learned one important lesson: You can always buy what you want at the "super sale" price. Nine times out of ten, that low great price is still available, "just for you." Why? Because they want your business. Even if they won't sell it to you at the price they were offering, you can always get it somewhere else. Don't give in to the pressure that you have to "buy now or pay *more* later!" Never let anyone bully you into believing that you have to buy anything right *now*.

9. *Use layaway or prepayment plans instead of credit.* Credit-savvy consumers know all too well that the best way to use credit sometimes is to not use it at all. Many stores are getting back to the tradition of layaway that was created years ago. With layaway, you put down a deposit and continue to pay toward your purchase — without incurring any interest charges. When you make your final payment, the store sends you your merchandise.

I've seen several great examples of layaway plans recently. Jostens, the manufacturers of class rings, offers a five-month layaway payment plan for high school and college class rings. And I attended a boat show where they were selling Health Craft cookware — which you could buy on their 3- or 10-month "warehouse plans." With the warehouse plans, you send in your monthly payments and each time you pay for one set of the cookware, they send that set of cookware to you. Once you make your final payment, you receive your final set of cookware.

10. *Steer away from "monthly payment options" for goods and services you buy, and make your purchases based on the <u>total</u> price.* It's always easier to buy something for "just three easy payments of $9.95" than it is to buy something for $25.95. But payment plans come with a price. That same item you could pay for in one payment of $25.95 will cost you $29.85 — nearly 15% more!

* * *

As you can see, it takes very little time to become a credit-savvy consumer — but the knowledge you gain could save you hundreds, even thousands of dollars, *every year*. First master some of the ins and outs of credit. Then start exploring some of the ways you can completely break the debt cycle that causes you to always worry about money. To help you get started, I've included some tips for breaking the debt cycle. These tips are excerpted from my book *Break the Debt Cycle — For Good!*.

Many of the ten tips you're about to read are based on sound prosperity principles. I encourage you to try all the ones you can today. Each month, stretch your comfort zone just a little, adding a new tip or two. You'll be pleasantly surprised to discover that these tips can actually help you break the debt cycle once and for all. Using these tips, you not only become debt-free, but you can actually develop a whole new way of thinking about money and credit and debt.

While you're paying off your remaining debts and building up a savings account for your new secured credit card (see Chapter 4), you have a few months to put these tips to work for you. You can become debt-free and *stay* debt-free if you follow these practical and metaphysical tips.

Bottom line, money is energy. Nothing less, nothing more. It does not have any power to control our actions — only our thoughts control our actions. Our thoughts about money usually fall in one of three stages. At the bottom is where you'll find most of us. This is where we spend our energy and time worrying about and talking about money problems. Where we spend most of our time saying things like *"I'm not going to have enough money to..."*

You can take the first step toward breaking the debt cycle by elevating your thinking. You can start elevating your thinking to the next stage *by setting goals for yourself.* This second stage is where we spend energy and time saying things like, *"I want to achieve this goal I've set, BUT I've got these money problems..."* If you're already at this stage, congratulate yourself. You're one step closer to permanent prosperity already.

You'll reach the third and highest stage once you make a committed effort to put the following ten tips to use in your life. When you've reached this stage, you'll find yourself saying things like, *"I have this goal, and it may be a very tiny goal, but it is my goal, and this is the next step I'll take to make this goal a reality."*

For example, let's say you're worried right now about meeting this month's mortgage or rent payment. Your goal is to come up with enough money to pay the mortgage or rent by the date it's due. You're on your way. Several of the tips below will immediately generate cash on hand to help you make your goal a reality. Other tips will help you build a foundation underneath you, so that more cash will come to you.

Ten Tips For Breaking the Debt Cycle — For Good!

I encourage you to start putting these ten tips to use in your life TODAY. Work toward progress, not perfection. Don't beat yourself up if you can't do everything at once. Take it a step at a time and keep moving forward. Above all else, know that YOU ARE PROSPEROUS!

1. *Free up the trapped prosperity in your life.* Release things that take up "space" in your life. Friends who sap your energy and provide nothing in return. Books, clothes, food — what are you stockpiling that you don't use? Look at everything you haven't used in over a year and find a way to sell it, give it away or trade it in.

Grab four empty boxes. Label them "Keep," "Trash," "Charity," and "Hold." Then take one drawer, one shelf, one box at a time. Set a timer for 15 minutes and go to it. When the timer goes off, immediately take the Trash box out to the trash. Put the Charity box into your car so it can go to charity immediately. Put everything in the Keep box where it belongs. Finally, stick the Hold box in a nearby closet. After you've decluttered your house, go back to the Hold boxes and decide where these items actually belong: Keep, Trash, or Charity.

2. *Pay what you can now.* If you have debts to pay, and you have savings, don't withhold money and say, "I'll pay these debts later, when I have more money so I don't have to touch my savings." Free up that money; put it into the universe. You can't get a flow of money coming in to you unless you have a flow of money going out. Pay what you can pay today, even if you can't pay the whole bill right now.

3. Release people from their debts to you. If you have lent money in the past, or extended credit, and you know that the chances for you ever getting that money back are remote, release the borrowers from their debt to you. Call or write them and say, *"I want you to know that I've decided to consider this money a gift to you. I am freeing you from any obligation to repay this money, ever, and I hope you'll accept this gift with all my love, and do the same for someone who owes you money."* You then make it possible for that money or more to come to you.

4. See the highest good for everyone. When you're in a situation where you think, *"they're going to try to rip me off"* affirm *"I see the highest good for both of us."* Then know this person will do right by you.

5. Give thanks for your debts. When you pay your debts, hold them one by one in your hand and give thanks for whatever that debt represents. *"Thank you Universe for Cable Television, which enables us as a family to watch movies together at home." "Thank you Universe for this dental bill, which took away the pain in my mouth." "Thank you Universe for this mortgage, which lets us live in this home we love."*

6. Don't brag about what you plan to accomplish or your prosperity. Instead, imagine it as accomplished, then go about your daily business, putting the stepping stones in place for your pathway to your goal. Then, once you've accomplished your goal, go inside yourself and give thanks for your abundance. And give back to those who have helped you achieve your prosperity.

7. Don't let pride stand in the way of your prosperity. You can be your own worst enemy if you refuse to accept your prosperity in whatever form it takes. As you practice the laws of prosperity, people around you will suddenly start giving you things. Don't refuse these gifts as charity or acts of pity. They are the first evidence that your prosperous thinking is paying off. Joyfully accept these gifts. Stop yourself before you say, *"Oh you shouldn't have." "This is too expensive." "I couldn't possibly accept."* Practice accepting gifts graciously. *"Bless your heart!" "You're an angel!" "Thank you."*

8. *Be patient with yourself as you learn prosperity skills.* Don't be like the farmer who planted corn, then cut off all the tassels that appeared, because he was looking to grow EARS of corn, not tassels. Don't dismiss the results you get as weeds. Know that whatever grows in your life is for your highest good.

9. *Look for the lesson in experiences.* When a "negative" happens to us, it's usually a nudge to help us chose a better direction for our lives, for our growth. Don't waste your time and energy bemoaning an event. Stop and center yourself and figure out what you were meant to learn, how this event will help you achieve your goals. Don't ask, *"Why did this happen to me?"* Ask, *"What am I going to do about it?"*

10. *Let go of prejudices.* Don't spend time and energy worrying about others, or how others perceive you. Remember the old taunt, *"I'm rubber and you're glue... whatever you say bounces off me and sticks on you?"* The same goes for positive thoughts and words. Don't set yourself above anyone else, or love others "in spite of" their actions. Learn to love everyone unconditionally and that love will flow back to you tenfold.

You can be your own worst enemy in your search for abundance or you can be the best guide you've every had. The choice is entirely up to you! There are two books by Catherine Ponder that I highly recommend as great "starter reading" for any prosperity thinking. They are: *Prosperity Secrets of the Ages* and *Open Your Mind To Receive*.

Use Affirmations to Free Up the Prosperity In Your Life

Affirmations are positive statements, said either aloud or to yourself, that can help you turn the negative thoughts we all have about money into positive thoughts about money.

I had read Catherine Ponder's writings for several years, but I kept hitting a block in my prosperity along the way, a plateau. Then I read *Open Your Mind To Receive* and I discovered just how easily I sabotaged my own prosperity, by saying or thinking things like "you shouldn't have" or "I don't take charity" when people would do nice things for me. Or chalking up prosperous events to "luck" instead of to my inner spiritual strength.

It was amazing to see what a difference occurred when I started using this simple affirmation: I AM OPEN AND RE-CEPTIVE TO RECEIVING MY HIGHEST GOOD NOW.

Here's another affirmation that will help you when life seems to be getting out of control: I NOW HAVE ENOUGH TIME, ENERGY, MONEY AND WISDOM TO ACCOM-PLISH ALL THAT I DESIRE.

And one more, for those days when you feel as if nothing you do will ever be enough: I AM ENOUGH, I HAVE ENOUGH, I DO ENOUGH!

Last, but not least: I FREELY ACCEPT AND OFFER ABUNDANCE AND THERE IS ALWAYS ENOUGH!

I've found that if I take two minutes to sit and stare at the water, or a ticking clock, or whatever, and slow my breathing down and focus on my heartbeat, for the rest of my day I have all the time I need. This quiet time also gives me a chance to slow down the chatter in my brain so I can focus on what I really want to accomplish.

I encourage you to start using these affirmations in your life. Pick one and repeat it to yourself whenever you start to feel worried about your financial situation. You will soon find your money worries becoming fewer and fewer.

Should You Repay Discharged Debts Once You're Prosperous

You may be tempted, once you get back on your financial feet, to attempt to "make good" on the debts you discharged under bankruptcy. This is a natural reaction, but not necessarily the best action to take. Your account has already been written off by the creditor as a business loss. As a result, the creditor has closed your account, and it would create a paper nightmare to find a way to post a payment to your account.

A better course of action might be to donate the money you would have paid creditors. There are always worthy causes that could benefit from your desire to repay your debts. Of course, if you win the lottery and can make a lump sum payment to your creditors, do what you feel is right for you.

Finally, let's look at how you can make your thoughts about money even more productive, using a technique I call "GoalGetting."

Using GoalGetting to Change the Way You Think About Money

What we learn about money is often heavily rooted in how we were raised around money. My parents never *talked* about money — but they often *argued* about it. So I always thought of money as something very taboo. But, I've learned that we can change the habits we learned from our parents, just as we can change any other habit. So, let's get started changing the way you think about money.

The first step in changing the way you think about money is to develop the habit of GoalGetting. Many of us set goals — but few of us actually achieve our goals. In trying to learn why this was so, I discovered that few of us break down our goals into manageable steps. These small steps — something you do *today* toward achieving one of your goals — make the difference between *setting* and actually *getting*, or achieving, your goal.

Sit down in a quiet place and think about what is most important to you. What do you want for yourself and your family — where do you want to be? Start with figuring out what you want and work backwards. Columnist George Will made the observation that "Europeans shop for what they want. Americans shop to DISCOVER what they want." So we Americans wind up spending much more money than we want to, trying to discover *what* we want.

So, what do you really want? What are your desires? Make a list for yourself of what things you really want. To pay off a $500 dental bill, to buy plane tickets to see your sister, to buy gardening supplies to start seeds indoors, to live for a year in Paris. Those are a few of my current goals — what do *you* really want?

Think about your goals, the things you want to do or have in your life. Is there a special function or date coming up that you want to buy something for? Then set a goal, a concrete goal, to make what you want a reality. Get out a notebook and grab a pen or pencil. This won't be painful at all, I promise! There are only six things you need to write down:

1. *The goal you want to achieve.* My goal is:

2. *The date you want to complete your goal by.* When do you need this to happen? Do you want to take your family to Disneyworld six months from now? I want to achieve my goal by this date: _____. It's important to set a deadline, and to make it as realistic as possible. Sometimes deadlines will have to be flexible, as you'll see in just a minute.

3. *How much money do you need to make your goal a reality?* This number may be far different once you start taking steps toward meeting your goals. In fact, you may find that your goal is far less expensive — and far more realistic — once you actually get costs for particular items or events.

Do your research. What will it cost to go to Disneyworld? How much would airfare be? Rental car? The cost of driving yourself? Hotel or campground? On-site lodging or off-site? Tickets to the theme parks? Food and souvenirs? I need this much money to make my goal a reality: $_____.

4. *How much do you have set aside right now that could go toward this goal?* Don't be discouraged if the answer is zero. All you need to know is what point you're starting from, as of today, to make your goal a reality. I have this much saved up: $_____.

5. How much do you still need to make your goal a reality?
I still need this much money $_____. (Start with the amount
in #3 and subtract the amount in #4.)

*6. How many paychecks (or weeks, if you get money in
spurts) are there between now and when I want to achieve my goal?*
I have this many weeks or paychecks before my goal: _____.

Now, divide the amount in #5 by the number in #6 to see
how much you need to pay toward this "bill" each week or each
paycheck so you can make your goal a reality.

Let's say that you want to take your family to Disneyworld six months from now. You know that airfare is going to run
you $100 a person if you can get a good fare. There's four of you,
so that's $400. Expect to pay $1,200 for passes to all the theme
parks, $300 for the car rental, $1,000 for the hotel, $1,400 for
food and souvenirs and an extra $500 for unexpected expenses.
That's $4,800. Divided by six months, that's $800 a month you'll
need to save to make your goal a reality. Eek!

Saving $800 a month for your fantasy vacation might not
leave anything left to pay your daily bills. Before you throw up
your hands and decide that taking the family to Disneyworld *isn't* a
reality, let's explore your options. First, you could postpone the
trip for another year. That way, you have 18 months (or 78
weeks) to save $4,800, at a rate of $266 per month. More reasonable? Broken down by week, that's just $61.54 a week.

Another option would be to see where you can pare down
the trip expenses to reduce the amount you need to save each
month. Could you drive instead of fly? What would gas, plus a
tune-up, plus "road food" cost? If you would rather fly and you'll
be only going to Disney theme parks, you could save money by

not getting a rental car. Everything at Disney is easily accessible through trams and buses.

You could also pare down your food bill by making a reservation for a hotel that has a kitchenette, and offers rooms that are like mini-apartments. *Residence Inn (800/331-3131)* is one good option. Or you could rent a week at a timeshare for a lower cost. One of the best timeshare discount rental companies is *TRI-WEST (800/341-4801)*.

Every day, get out your goal sheet and decide what *one* step you can take to make that goal a reality. Each night, at dinner, sit at the table and talk about what you want to be doing; what your goals are, what you did today to make progress toward reaching at least one of those goals. Give thanks and share your gratitude for what you have in your lives and for everything that is about to appear. Almost magically, what you desire will appear — as long as you take at least one step, every day, toward getting your goal.

Using The GoalGetter Sheet To Your Best Advantage

The bottom line is: Your goals won't come to you. You have to go out and get them, taking one step at a time, one action at a time to make your goals appear in your life. Others will comment on your "instant success" and how easy things come to you once you start using the *GoalGetter Sheet.*

The quickest and easiest way to achieve your dreams is to write them down. Make a list of the goals you want to achieve in your life. Then, each week, look over your goals. Decide which three goals you want to make progress on this week. Write down the action you'll take on that goal.

Keep your actions down to three a week at first. I don't want you to get so gung-ho that you burn yourself out before you can achieve any of your goals. Three actions a week will get you started. Whether you're trying to achieve a short-term goal for this month, or a long-term goal for years from now, the *GoalGetter Sheet* on page 86 will help you get there.

To get you started, use the *GoalGetter Sheet* to write down your top twelve goals. Then decide what one step you can take today toward achieving one of your goals. Then pick two other steps you can take this week toward your goals.

Get Your Whole Family Involved In GoalGetting

The quickest and easiest way to get your whole family involved in GoalGetting is to make sure that one of the goals you're trying to achieve is a family goal. Make a game out of seeing where you can save money. Sit down and set out a family goal — maybe you've always wanted to go see the Grand Canyon, or go to Disneyworld, or have season tickets to the WNBA.

Whatever your goal is, make sure it's a goal that everyone is excited about. Use the questions above to help you figure out how much it will cost you to achieve your goal. Then work together to free up the money in your everyday expenses, to start setting money aside to achieve your goal.

You can designate half the money you save toward debt repayment and half toward your goal, if you still have debt to repay. This way, you make progress in getting out of debt *and* you make progress toward achieving your family goal!

You'll be amazed at how quickly your kids — and you — realize that you don't really want the things that are "impulse buys." Especially if you sit down together and say, *"Let's see...we can have these extra premium channels on cable, for instance, or we can put $15 in our dream jar."*

Be sure to stick pictures of what you want for your goal on the outside of the jar, so you can daydream about achieving your goal!

Once you're comfortable with using the *GoalGetter Sheet,* and once you've gotten into the habit of doing at least three things a week toward your goals, gradually increase your pace until you're doing one action toward one of your goals every day.

Every day, ask yourself, *"What one thing can I do toward one of my goals today?"* Then do that one thing. If you do more than one thing that day, great, but make sure that you do at least one thing every day.

One way to discipline yourself so you don't get burned out is to force yourself to *only* do one thing a day toward your goals for 21 days. By then, you'll be going bonkers that you can't make more progress — but you'll also be in the habit of looking to see how the action you're taking today will help you meet your goals.

GoalGetter Sheet

My Goals Are....	Action For This Goal This Week
Example: Be financially independent in three years.	*Call 800-507-9244 for the date of the next **Break the Debt Cycle — For Good!** seminar.*
1.	
2.	
3.	
4.	
5.	
6.	
7.	
8.	
9.	
10.	
11.	
12.	

Chapter 3: Action Items

1. Make a commitment to yourself to follow the rules that credit-savvy consumers use. Once you start "acting-as-if" you're a credit-savvy consumer, you'll soon discover that you've actually *become* a credit-savvy consumer.

2. Use one of the *Ten Tips For Breaking the Debt Cycle — For Good!* today. Keep using that tip every day and every few days add another tip until you're using all ten tips every day.

3. Start saying one of the affirmations in this chapter — or an affirmation you've created for yourself — every day, any time you find yourself worrying about money.

4. Write down your goals, for every areas of your life.

5. Break one of your goals into manageable financial chunks so you can start to make it a reality.

6. Use the *GoalGetter Sheet* to write down and keep track of the daily action you can take toward achieving one of your goals.

chapter 4

When You're Ready to Start Rebuilding Your Credit

Are you worried that you'll never, ever get a credit card again after your bankruptcy? Or are you glad to be rid of credit cards forever — and swear that you'll never touch another piece of credit card plastic as long as you live?

You're not alone, no matter how you feel about credit cards. But credit cards offer you a very valuable way to rebuild your credit history after bankruptcy. By rebuilding your credit history, you can qualify for the same low interest rates on car loans and mortgages as other consumers do.

Shortly after I declared bankruptcy, I received a generous offer from a company to rebuild my credit and get a new credit card. Imagine the relief I felt! For about $50, I could qualify for a VISA or MasterCard. But here's what really was being offered:

For my $50, I received a plastic "Universal" credit card — which was accompanied by a catalog of overpriced merchandise. In order to qualify for a MasterCard or VISA, I first had to "charge" a total of $3,000 on my "Universal" credit card. The company charged a hefty interest rate — about 17% back then. I bought merchandise from their catalog at an incredible markup — and even paid a sizable $80 "annual fee" a year later.

Finally, I became "eligible" for a VISA or MasterCard. My eligibility consisted of a list of companies that offered secured credit cards. What a scam!

Beware of companies that send you literature on getting a new credit card right after bankruptcy, including companies that promise "offshore credit cards." These companies are frauds. These companies are either complete cons or they're merchandising companies in business to get your money. Don't give your money to them.

If a credit card offer sounds too good to be true, it is. Run the other way as fast as you can. If you get a telephone call, letter or postcard offering you a credit card you "can't be turned down for," call your local Better Business Bureau, State Attorney General's office and/or your consumer affairs office for the company's history. You'll probably discover some pretty nasty problems that the company's representative didn't share with you. Read the fine print in any literature or forms. There are a lot of these companies out there, trying to prey on your fears about never being able to have a credit card after you've declared bankruptcy.

Three such offers are the *U.S. Charge Card* from ShopSmart, Inc. (which was listed as a defendent in an "Advance-Fee Loan Fraud Crackdown), the *RESOURCE Card* from Financial Services Network, and *MONEYCARD*, from the financial division of CMM (which is being marketed over the Internet).

Your first hint that the *MONEYCARD* is *not* a real credit card, even though it touts a $1,000 unsecured credit line, is a fact which they state right up front: Bank Affiliation: NONE. All *genuine* credit cards are affiliated with an issuing bank. Don't give any company money for a credit card unless you know what bank is issuing the card *and* you've checked with the Better Business Bureau to make sure the bank is legitimate. And please don't get taken in by these "offshore" guaranteed credit card offers. They're scams, pure and simple.

To get the *MONEYCARD*, you need to pay an up-front membership fee of $149.95. They try to suck you in with promises of cash advances on your card, and they tell you that one of your "membership benefits" is that you will be "processed for an unsecured VISA or MasterCard with a credit line of up to $1,000."

In an aside, in teeny type, they tell you that the "processing" you get is simply this: they give you an application form from *Ocean Independent Bank* or *Cross Country Bank* for one of their unsecured credit card. This wouldn't be so laughable if *Cross Country* and *Ocean Independent* offered a halfway decent credit card — but both cards charge a $100 application fee and a $50 annual fee. To add insult to injury, *Cross Country* and *Ocean Independent* don't even give you a grace period on their cards, and you'll only qualify for a credit line of $350, not the $1,000 *MONEYCARD* teases you with.

The *RESOURCE Card* also really made me laugh. The interest rate they charge is "based on your personal situation" — which you know means "it will be really high." How high? Well, the computer message on the 800-number won't tell you and you can't get a live person to talk to you. You have to pay the $48 membership fee before you can even find out what the interest rate is. Thanks, but no thanks! Don't give any company money for a credit card unless they tell you *in writing* what their interest rate is.

The *RESOURCE* Card computer message also tells you that you can get your own "collateralized MasterCard" — even if you have poor credit. What is a "collateralized MasterCard?" It's a secured credit card. What you get from *RESOURCE* is a list of secured credit cards, and you already have the best of them, the only ones that help you rebuild your credit, right here in this book.

Beware also of "guaranteed" credit card offers, especially those that require you to pay a fee, usually $100 or more. Think about it for a second — why would you pay some stranger $100 for something that your gut tells you is too good to be true? Because you want to rebuild your credit, that's why. And these guys know that you're worried about the negative affect your bankruptcy will have on your ability to get credit. That's why they prey on newly bankrupt folks.

Companies make these offers sound like the $100 or more you pay them is the deposit for a secured credit card. But what you'll really get is a list of credit card companies who offer secured credit cards — the same list you can get from Bankcard Holders of America for $4 or FREE from this book.

Instead of sending that $100 to a company that makes grand promises to you, write out the $100 check to a good secured credit card lender like Capital One, which only requires a $100 minimum in order to get a secured credit card. You'll rebuild your credit much faster that way.

Learn from my mistake, please. I fell for one of the "merchandising card" scams. I paid over $3,000 for a list that you — anyone actually — can get for $4. But I'm actually including detailed information on the best secured credits cards in this book, so this information is actually *free* to you!

For the absolute most current list, you can send a $4 check or money order to Bankcard Holders of America, 524 Branch Drive, Salem, VA 24153. Be sure to specify in your letter that you want the *secured* credit card list. You can also get a free list of all lenders who issue secured credit cards on-line, at http://www.bankrate.com. If you decide to get the most recent list, be sure to run the cards through the tests in this chapter to make sure that you're getting the best secured credit card for you. Before I dive into the details on the best way to get a new, secured credit card, I urge you to get only *one* credit card for your personal use. If you need to keep business expenses separate, then *two* credit cards are the most you will need.

There really is no need to have more than two credit cards. One credit card with a small credit limit will do wonders to help rebuild your credit history. Keep this one card, and over time, as you pay your bill in full each month, the creditor will raise your credit limit. Once they raise your credit limit, I encourage you to continue to charge only what you can afford to pay off in full each month. Otherwise, creditors will think that you're repeating the same debt cycle over again.

Speaking from experience, too much available credit after bankruptcy might not be a wise idea. The debt can creep up on your faster than you know. Luckily, if you find yourself in trouble down the road, after the creditor has increased your credit limit above and beyond your secured deposit amount, you can get back on track quickly and easily. With one simple phone call and a follow-up letter, you can reduce your credit card debt by the amount of your security deposit. Simply ask to have the account closed and have the security deposit used to pay toward the balance you owe on the card. Especially if you're like me, and ran up credit card debt in the past, this is a nice safety valve.

Shopping For The Best Secured Credit Card

A secured credit card looks and acts like a regular MasterCard or VISA. The only difference? You deposit money as collateral for your credit line rather than having the company extend you credit. The money is yours and is deposited in a savings account where it earns interest like any other savings account. You can enjoy all the benefits of a regular MasterCard or VISA, including the greatest luxury of all: re-establishing your credit history.

As long as you handle your credit responsibly — by not overspending and by paying what you owe on time every month — your credit report will shine brighter and brighter every month. Within two years you may find that you've got sparkling credit, an unsecured credit card, and your deposit back, plus interest.

But before I throw more credit card gobbledy-gook at you, it's important to know a few credit card terms. You'll find them in every credit card application.

Adjusted Balance. This is the best way a creditor can calculate your finance charges. Unfortunately, it's not the most common way. (See *Average Daily Balance*, below.) With this method, your creditor subtracts any payments you made from the balance you owed at the end of the previous billing period. Your creditor does not include any new purchases. In addition, your creditor may not include unpaid finance charges when they calculate your adjusted balance.

Annual Fee. Every year you own your credit card, you may pay a fee to the issuing bank for having your account. Annual fees hover around $35, but can jump as high as $80. Occasionally, you'll find a bank that charges no annual fee, but that's not necessarily a good thing. You may end up paying an extra high interest rate, or extra transaction fees instead. Likewise, a higher annual fee could be offset by no transaction fees and no cash advance fees.

Average Daily Balance. This is how most credit cards calculate your finance charge. Every day, your credit card issuer will total the beginning balance on your account and subtract any payments credited to your account that day. The creditor may also add new purchases and cash advances to the balance. These daily balances are then added up and divided by the number of days in the billing cycle, to arrive at the "average daily balance."

Credit Limit, Line of Credit, or Credit Line. This is the maximum you can charge to your credit card. For a secured credit card your credit limit equals, or is a percentage of, your savings. The best cards offer a credit line of 100%-200% of your security deposit. You can find secured cards with larger limits, but make sure you can afford both the security deposit that a large credit limit requires and the bills you can rack up.

Exceeding Your Credit Limit Fee. Going over your credit limit can cost you. Some banks charge you if you exceed your credit limit, some don't — these costs can range from $5-$35.

Grace Period. Your grace period is the number of days (usually 25-30 days) you have to repay your balance without paying an additional finance charge. Some banks expect you to pay immediately — they give you no grace period. Most others will give you a grace period to repay your purchases, but none to repay your cash advances. Grace periods for cash advances are harder to find (they're listed as "no cash advance fee").

Interest Rate. If you don't pay off your balance each month, you'll be charged a percentage of the balance remaining on your account. A low interest rate is best for you if you don't think you'll pay your balance in full at the end of each month. The interest, or finance charge, is the cost you pay for using the bank's money to make your purchases now. As long as your credit card has a grace period, and you pay off your balance in full each month, you won't have to pay any interest on your purchases. The interest rate is called the *"Annual Percentage Rate."*

Late Payment Fee. Pay late, and you'll be charged an additional $10-$25 each month as a late payment fee.

Minimum Deposit. This is the least amount of money that the credit card's issuing bank requires you to deposit into a savings account to secure your credit limit. You won't be able to touch this money until you close your account or switch to an unsecured card. Choose a minimum deposit you can afford.

Transaction Fee. Every time you use your credit card's special features — like withdrawing money from an ATM — you'll be charged a transaction fee. These fees vary.

What's The Best Secured Credit Card For You?

Like regular credit cards, secured credit cards come in all flavors. Some charge high annual fees, some charge interest rates varying from moderate to outrageous, and some allow no grace period while others allow 30-35 days.

So how do you find the best secured credit card for you? For starters, you need to know what's important to you in a card.

Do you want a low net interest rate? *Metropolitan Credit Union* (11.35%) is the best around.

Do you want a low annual fee? Then you might want to go with *American Pacific* or *First Union* (both $35).

Do you need a high credit limit? *American Pacific* and *First Union* both offer credit limits up to $15,000.

Do you want to earn a higher interest rate on your savings deposit? *Capital One* (2.59%), *Metropolitan* (2.55%) and *American Pacific* (2.50%) offer good returns on your savings deposit.

The best secured card for you will depend on what you want out of the card. No matter what factors are most important to you, please make sure your secured card meets these criteria:

First, look for a minimum deposit you can afford to be without for awhile — some banks let you open up a secured credit card account for as little as $99. You can always deposit more money and increase your credit limit, but it's best to start with an amount you can afford to set aside in a savings account.

Second, look for the card's grace period. I recommend picking a card that offers at least a 25-day grace period.

Third, look for the best interest rate. Cards calculate their interest rates one of four ways:

1. *A flat interest rate.* Usually this will seem pretty steep — 19% - 21% is pretty standard. But don't be fooled — other cards' rates may be even higher.

2. *The federal discount rate plus a set flat rate.* You can find the federal discount rate by looking in any copy of ***The Wall Street Journal*** under the heading "Money Rates" in the "C" section of the paper. You can also find the federal discount rate on-line, by going to http://www.bog.frb.fed.us/releases/H15/update. The federal discount rate is listed as "discount window borrowing." The federal discount rate is the rate the Federal

Reserve Banks charge your bank. Currently this rate is 6%. So a card that charges the federal discount rate plus 5% charges just 11% — a fabulous interest rate!

3. *The prime rate plus a set flat rate.* You can find the prime rate in the same place as you find the federal discount rate – – under "Money Rates" in *The Wall Street Journal.* To find the prime rate on-line, go to http://www.bog.frb.fed.us/releases/H15/ update. The prime rate is listed as "bank prime loan." The prime rate is the rate the nation's 30 largest banks charge corporations when they borrow money. The current rate is 9.50%. So a card that charges the prime rate plus 13.50% actually has a rate of 23%. Ouch!

4. *The London Interbank Offered Rate (LIBOR) plus a flat rate.* The LIBOR is also published in the Money Rate section of *The Wall Street Journal.* You can also find the LIBOR on-line, by going to http://www.bog.frb.fed.us/releases/H15/update. The LIBOR rate is listed as "Eurodollar deposits (London)." The LIBOR is the average rate the five major London banks charge other banks. There are four different LIBOR rates. Credit card issuers commonly use *the three month rate* which is currently 6.7%. So a card that charges the LIBOR plus 5.5% actually has a rate of 12.2% — not bad at all!

Choosing The Best Secured Credit Card

Use the deposit amount, grace period and interest rate as your first three screening tools, to narrow down your choices to several secured cards. First, check with your bank or credit union to see if they offer a secured credit card that meets the above criteria. If they don't then look at these select few cards closely for the following options that are the most important to you.

1. *Matching credit limit increases.* Some cards will increase your credit line by twice the amount you deposit, once you've proven that you're a good credit risk. For example, if you deposit $500, your actual credit line increase may be $1,000.

2. *Ability to switch to an unsecured card.* Some cards, after one or two years, will give you back your secured deposit so that you can invest it elsewhere. This is a wonderful option.

3. *A gradually lower interest rate.* Some cards, after a few years of good credit history, will lower the interest rate you're charged. Of course, if you get a lower rate card to begin with, there's less allure to this feature.

4. *A high yield on your deposit.* Secured credit cards pay different yields on the money in your secured savings account. Some pay as little as 2.5%, while others pay as much as 7%.

But don't just jump at the highest yielding savings account or the lowest interest rate card. Instead, subtract what you're being paid from what you're being charged to get your *net interest rate.*

For example: a card charging 9.75% and paying you 2.5% actually charges a net interest rate of 7.25%. And a card charging you 22.3% and paying you 7% actually charges a net interest rate of 15.3%.

However, don't just automatically conclude that a higher yield is a bad thing. For example, a card that charges 18.9% and pays you 4.5% is actually charging you 14.4% — almost a full percentage point less than the card paying 7% on your savings!

Make Sure Your Credit Card Is Helping You Rebuild Your Credit

Since you goal is to re-establish your credit, read this chapter thoroughly and pick the one credit card that you feel would be best for you. Then apply for that one card. Don't apply for several cards at once or you'll get a bunch of new inquiries on your credit reports. Too many inquiries make creditors nervous — and less likely to extend credit to you.

Above all else, make sure the credit card company issuing your card meets these two rules:

1. *The issuing bank reports your payment history every month to the three major credit bureaus.* If your credit isn't reported regularly to CBI/Equifax, Experian and TransUnion, then you're wasting your time with this card. When you're ready to take out a car loan or a mortgage, you want your good payment history to shine through.

2. *The issuing bank must keep your secured status confidential — only you and the bank know your card is secured, not the credit bureaus.* A secured credit card can only help you re-establish credit if the credit bureau does not know your savings act as collateral for your credit.

When a bank lists a credit card as secured on your credit report, it means that other creditors immediately know that the card is not really issued as a credit — it's secured by your collateral, your security deposit. This won't help you build a positive credit history, so make sure that the secured card you select is NOT listed as secured on your credit reports.

These two conditions won't jump out at you on all applications because they may not be there. Banks aren't required to tell you, so make sure you ask. In addition, banks often change their policies. *Orchard Bank*, for instance, was one of my top picks for secured cards. Now, however, they do't make the grade because they no longer report your account to the credit bureaus until your card is converted to unsecured. And *Key Bank & Trust*, which issued my favorite secured card, no longer issues secured credit cards at all.

When it comes to specific cards, *First National Bank of Marin*, for instance, is a card to stay away from. *Marin* reports the secured status of your credit card, violating rule #2. The application looks like all the rest — from its annual fee to its secured status, and your good payment habits will be reported to credit bureaus, but so, unfortunately, will your secured credit status.

If you get a *First National Bank of Marin* secured credit card, your credit history could be spotless and yet as far as a future creditor is concerned you haven't been "accepted as a good credit risk" — because the card is listed as being secured by your deposit. The credit card company isn't assuming any real risk.

A few more cards you might want to steer away from are cards from *Amalgamated, Banco Popular, Bank of America, Bank of Hoven, California Commerce Bank, Citibank* (they don't even report that you *have* a credit card, until it's no longer secured!), *Chase* (they won't even give you a secured card until your bankruptcy is seven years old!), *Elan, First National Bank* (high fees), *People's Bank, Pentagon Federal Credit Union, Sterling* (processing fees), *Union Plus, Washington Mutual, Whitney National* (only reports to Equifax), *Wells Fargo Bank* and *Zions*.

In addition, *J.C. Penney* offers a secured card as well — but again, they report your account as being secured by your deposit, which doesn't help you rebuild your credit history. In addition, J.C. Penney tries to entice you to max out your card by offering an additional 10% discount on all purchases made the *first* day you use your card.

Other card issuers, like *United National* and *Providian Bank* don't make the grade because they have no grace period. You begin accruing interest charges the minute you charge something. Even if you pay your bill in full each month, you'll still wind up paying interest!

Unlike these cards, all the cards listed on the following pages meet my stringent requirements. Check out the chart on page 129 for more specifics on each card.

When you find the best card for you, call the toll-free number provided to request an application. You should receive your application within two weeks, if not a few days. Fill out all spaces on the application. Blank areas will delay processing or disqualify you completely. If you have a co-applicant, his or her information must also be complete — and don't forget to sign the application. Sometimes, you'll have to sign in several places.

Most banks let you deposit your money using a personal check, cashier's check or money order — whatever suits you. Personal checks generally take an extra two weeks to clear, so if you need a credit card quickly, you're better off using a cashier's check or money order. Most banks also have a few general requirements for all secured credit card applicants. Before bombarding your credit report with inquiries, check to see if you qualify. You'll usually find these requirements:

• You must be at least 18 years old,
• You must be a U.S. citizen, or a permanent U.S. resident (depending on the credit card),
• For the past 6 months, you must have paid all of your bills on time,
• You must have no Federal Tax Liens outstanding.

Your bankruptcy won't count against you with the credit card issuers included in this book — as long as your debts have been discharged, and you have no outstanding liens against you.

Top Secured Credit Cards

Every card has its own additional requirements, and you may or may not be eligible, depending on your situation.

American Online/American Pacific Bank *(800/610-1201 or 503/ 749-1200; www.apbank.com).* To get a VISA credit card quickly, call *American Pacific Bank*, unless you live in Wisconsin, where this card isn't available. You'll have your card in three weeks if you use a personal check. A cashier's check or money order can be processed in two weeks.

If you want your card even faster, you can make your deposit using a wire transfer and pay a transfer charge of $25, along with your security deposit. You'll get your card overnight, once you've been approved. Take a look at *American Pacific's* additional requirements:

• You must have at least a $10,000 annual income before taxes, and provide a copy of your current paycheck stub;

• You must have a street address (you can use a P.O. Box for your statements after your account is set up), and a telephone in your name.

• Your bankruptcy must be discharged (if filed in the past 12 months, include a copy of your discharge papers). A Chapter 13 bankruptcy must be at least six months old.

Mail your completed application with your minimum deposit of $400 (or $1,000 for businesses).

Your credit limit will match your savings deposit, and you can increase your limit at any time by sending a check for $100 or more. Be sure to write "Credit Limit Increase" on your check to make sure that *American Pacific* doesn't mistake your check for a regular payment. This card offers a 25-day grace period.

After 9 months, if you've kept your account current, *American Pacific* will increase your credit limit 25% with no additional deposit from you. After your account has been current for 36 months, *American Pacific* will convert your secured credit card into an unsecured card, and you get your deposit back.

Don't have a steady income? Not to worry! *American Pacific* also offers a VISA for people who are self-employed or can't verify their income. To apply for their "No-Income Secured VISA Card," you'll need to make a security deposit that is 120% of your requested credit line. For example, if you want a $500 credit line, you'll need to deposit $600. The maximum credit line for this card is $1,000. In all other respects, this credit card is just like their regular secured credit card.

Capital One (800/548-4593; www.capitalone.com). *Capital One* is one of the leading issuers of secured credit cards these days, and offers several different secured credit cards with various credit limits. All their cards have a 25-day grace period.

You could be eligible for their $100 deposit/$500 credit line or their standard $200 deposit/$300 credit line.

The best offer you'll find in secured credit cards is *Capital One's* $100 deposit/$500 credit line. However, I urge you to be very careful with this type of card, since you can rack up some pretty good charges without any security deposit to fall back on if money gets tight down the road.

The additional requirements you must meet to be eligible for a *Capital One* secured credit card are:

- You cannot be a resident of Maine, North Carolina, Vermont or Wisconsin;
- You cannot be currently incarcerated;
- You can have no history of credit card fraud;
- You cannot be subject to back-up IRS withholding.

On the *Capital One* application, you will see a line for your employer's name and telephone number, but you do not have to have a job to get a *Capital One* secured credit card. Fill in "not applicable" if you are unemployed or self-employed.

Using a personal check instead of a cashier's check or money order makes a difference in how quickly your credit line is increased. Your credit line increases in 18 days if you use your check versus three days for a cashier's check or money order.

Capital One will review your account every 12 months (you may have to request it) and will — if your credit is good — increase your credit line without requiring you to deposit more money. In 30 months, if your account remains in good standing, the savings requirement may be dropped altogether, converting your secured card to unsecured. The credit limit on your secured account cannot exceed $1,000.

The only drawback that I can see to *Capital One's* card is that if you get in over your head, and want to close your account, you may have a harder time getting your secured deposit back until you've first paid off the card's balance, in full.

First Consumers National Bank *(503/520-8200 or 800/876-3262; www.fcnb.com).* Your *First Consumers* deposit can be as little as $100 and your credit line will be 100%-300% of the amount you deposit. *FCNB* has the following additional requirements:

- Your gross monthly income must be at least $1,000;
- You must have a telephone in your home; and a street address (not a P.O. Box);
  - Your bankruptcy must have been discharged or filed more than 12 months ago (include a copy of your discharge papers for faster processing.)
  - Any Federal Tax Liens must be satisfied or released. (Include a copy of your lien release papers to speed up processing.)

FCNB's grace period is about 30 days. As long as this account is secured, your credit line cannot exceed $2,500. Your account can convert to unsecured in as little as one year. However, this card is not available in North Carolina or Vermont.

The interest rate on *FCNB's* card is fixed at 18.9%. When interest rates are low and looking to rise, you're better off having a secured credit card that offers a fixed interest rate, unless you're planning on paying off your balance in full each month.

First Premier Bank *(800/987-5521 or 605/357-3458; www.firstpremier.com). First Premier* charges a fixed interest rate of 18.9% on balances up to $1,000; 16.9% if your balance exceeds $1,000. They pay no interest on your savings and their annual fee is kind of steep: $45 plus a $1/month "participation fee," which works out to a $57 annual fee. One nice perk: they only report late payments when they're more than 60 days past due.

First Premier has no application fee and the minimum deposit is $200. For rush processing, you can fax your application to *First Premier* (605/357-3445) and wire your security deposit via Western Union or a bank wire. All the details are included with your application. They'll periodically review your payment history. If your payments are on time and you pay more than the minimum amount due each month, they'll generally convert you to an unsecured card after 12-18 months.

First Union *(800/413-7914; www.firstunion.com). First Union* offers a 30 day grace period. They charge an interest rate of prime plus 9.9% (with a minimum of 18.9%). Your minimum deposit must be $400, but you can have a large credit line of up to $15,000, if you're willing to tie up that much cash in a savings account earning 1.49%!

Still, they do make the grade in the areas that count. They report to all three major credit bureaus, and report your card as unsecured. Additional deposits to your account can be made in $100 increments, so you can gradually build up your credit line.

<u>Metropolitan Credit Union</u> (200 Revere Beach Parkway, Chelsea, MA 02510; 800-654-7728, www.metrocreditunion.org) was the first credit union that passed my strict tests. The minimum deposit is $500, they offer a 25-day grace period, the interest rate is a very low 12.9% and they pay 2.75% on your deposit — so your net interest rate is 10.15%. Who says newly bankrupt people have to pay through the nose to get credit? When it comes to interest rates, *Metropolitan's* secured card offers the best interest rate around. You can convert your secured account to an unsecured account in 12-15 months, if your account is in good standing.

Metropolitan's secured credit card is a nice card to use if you need access to your deposit, but want to rebuild your credit. The cash advance fee is just 95-cents per transaction.

Want your card in a hurry? *Metropolitan* offers two different rush packages. You can pay an extra $20 for two day turnaround or pay an extra $32 for one day turnaround. All around, *Metropolitan* offers a winning card.

Others who use *Metropolitan's* secured credit card rave about their customer service. One woman fell behind on her payments when her child fell ill. She said Metropolitan was wonderful to deal with and eager to work with her to get caught up on her bill. As with any creditor, if you fall behind, call the creditor right away instead of waiting for them to call you. Creditors are much more likely to work with you, instead of against you, if you're being proactive and taking steps to get back on track.

Need A Higher Limit On Your Secured Credit Card

When you need to increase your credit limit on your secured card, you don't have to make additional deposits to your savings account. Instead, you can "prepay" your credit card bill.

Your credit limit would still be the same, but you would have a credit on your card, making it possible for you to actually purchase more with your credit card.

For example, say you have a secured credit card with a $200 credit line and you need to charge $450 worth of travel expenses this month. If you prepay $250 to your card, and your balance is zero, you would have a credit line of $200, plus a credit to your account of $250. This gives you a total of $450 worth of available credit this month. You're not actually increasing your credit limit, but you are actually increasing your ability to make purchases this month.

Can You Get An Unsecured Credit Card After Bankruptcy?

Your immediate reaction to my suggestion to get a secured credit card might be *"why should I get a secured card instead of an unsecured card, when I'm getting offers for unsecured credit cards left and right?"* Secured credit cards have gotten a bad rap, because most don't help you rebuild your credit history. That's why I was very selective in researching the secured credit cards — to make sure that all the cards listed in this book are working *for* you and not *against* you.

When you use one of the secured credit cards I've listed in this book, no one else will know that the credit card is secured except *you*. Financially, secured credit cards offer you a better deal than any of the unsecured cards you're likely to run into after your bankruptcy.

Now is the time to create some new credit habits. You don't need a big credit line in order to buy the things you want now — instead, you're learning how to plan for the purchases you want to make, so that you can have what you want when you want it, *without adding any new revolving debt.*

Companies That Offer
Unsecured Credit Cards After Bankruptcy

There are several companies that are making good money offering unsecured credit cards to people after their bankruptcy is discharged. Before you rush out and get in line for one of these cards, though, I want you to know that *I am not a fan of unsecured cards*. Especially not for unsecured cards being offered to folks who've recently gone bankrupt.

It doesn't surprise me that two of the companies offering these unsecured cards are solid companies that used to offer secured credit cards. They've discovered that there is an untapped market of people who feel secured credit cards carry a stigma — but as you've seen, the trick is to have the *right* secured credit card.

When you get a direct mail pitch for an unsecured credit card, it will probably promise a credit line of "Up to $1,000!" or "Up to $5,000!" Yes, if your income is $200,000 a year, you *might* qualify for a credit line that high. But chances are, if you send in your application fee, you'll find that you get an unsecured credit card back with a credit limit of $250-$300.

Orchard Bank now offers an *unsecured* VISA to people with bankruptcy on their records, with a $300 initial credit limit. You'll need a gross annual income of $12,000 to qualify. The interest rate for *Orchard's* unsecured credit card is 18.9% or Prime plus 9.75% (whichever is higher). You get a 30-day grace period, but the first year annual fee is a killer — $90! The annual fee drops to $45 from the second year on. *Orchard* will increase your limit regularly, as long as you're current.

Let's see how *Orchard's* unsecured card stacks up against, say, *Capital One's* secured card, shall we? The interest rate for *Orchard's* unsecured card is 18.9% or Prime plus 9.9% (whichever is higher). So your interest rate would be 18.9%. *Capital One,* meanwhile, is charging an interest rate of 19.8% and paying a yield of 2.59% on your security deposit, bringing your net interest rate down to 17.21%. And their annual fee is just $39.

Bottom line, you wind up paying 1.7% MORE to have an unsecured *Orchard Bank* credit card. Plus you pay an extra $51 the first year for the jacked-up annual fee, and an extra $6 every year after that. Financially, *Capital One's* secured card makes more sense than *Orchrd Bank's* unsecured card.

There are some other unsecured credit cards that you would also do well to steer away from. Most of them charge you such high up-front fees that you're in debt before you even receive your credit card! The VISA being offered by *Stutsman County State Bank* is one example. They offer you a $150 unsecured credit line. But, you pay a $98 processing fee and a $39 annual fee every year.

The good news is that both of these are charged to the credit card, so you don't have to pay them out of your pocket. The bad news is that once you pay the processing fee and the annual fee, you're left with an available credit line of $13 and a debt of $137! So you can't even use the credit card until you've paid down (or better yet, paid off) the $137.

First Premier also offers an unsecured credit card now, with a $250 credit limit. Like *Orchard, First Premier* charges a hefty

$89 processing fee, and a $89 annual fee. Right from the start, $178 of that $250 credit limit is already spent and racking up interest charges. Again, you would be much better off getting a secured card.

Another way unsecured cards will zap up you is by not offering you any grace period, which means you start paying interest on everything you charge from the minute you charge it.

One such card which has no grace period is *Providian*. I promise you, the secured cards listed in this book give you a much better way to reestablish your credit.

After you've had a good payment history with a secured credit card, you will eventually get offers for unsecured cards which don't require you to pay any money up-front. One excellent company, which originally gave me a $300 credit limit after my bankruptcy was seven years old, is *First North American National Bank*. After a year of paying off my credit card each month, they increased my credit limit to $600.

Eventually, I closed out my secured credit card accounts with *Key Bank and Trust*. I replaced them with the *First North American National Bank* with its $600 credit limit and an unsecured *Capital One* card with a $1,000 credit limit.

For me, I know that I wouldn't be able to pay off more than $1,600 over a two month period, so $1,600 in available credit meets my needs. How much credit do you need? You'll be surprised at how *little* credit you'll actually need — and you don't need to carry a balance from month to month in order to put new, positive credit information on your credit report. So be conservative when you estimate how much credit you'll need. I don't want you getting in debt over your head again, just as you're starting to get back on your feet.

Be especially on guard for any "pre-approved offers" for credit that show up in your mailbox. These days, "pre-approved" only means that you passed their first screening test, which is usually that you had an address. The fine print will tell you that they'll still check your credit report before you qualify. This only winds up putting a bunch of inquiries on your credit report — which future creditors will see as a sign that you're desperate to get your hands on more credit.

One way to avoid these temptations is to let the credit bureaus know that you do not want them selling your name to credit card companies or other lenders. To get your name removed from these mailing lists, send this letter to Equifax:

(Date)

Equifax Options
P.O. Box 740123
Atlanta, GA 30374-0123

Dear Sir/Madam:

I am writing to request that you remove my name from the mailing lists you provide to credit card companies and lenders.

Enclosed is the information you need to verify my request:

* [your complete name]
* [your full address]
* [your Social Security Number]

I understand that you will remove my name from your mailing lists and that you will share my request with Experian and TransUnion, so that my name will be removed from their mailing lists as well.

Sincerely,

[Your name]

If you need access to larger amounts of money throughout the month, you might want to look into getting a debit card, in addition to your secured credit card.

Are Debit Cards Good Or Bad

You can easily get a "debit" or "check" card from your bank that looks and acts like a credit card when you buy products or services. Most debit cards give you the convenience of a credit card while helping you create (and maintain) the discipline of spending only the cash you have, because the money is drawn out of your checking account.

When you get your debit card, it will usually have a VISA logo on it and look exactly like a VISA. The only difference, on some cards, is that the card says "check card" or "debit card" above the logo. Some debit cards have this notation, others don't.

You can use your debit card anywhere they take VISA (including the Olympics!). Instead of the money being taken out of your credit limit on a credit card, where you have to pay it back with interest, the charges you make using your debit card are subtracted directly from your checkbook.

With a debit card, you can place mail orders over the telephone, order concert tickets, eat at restaurants without having to carry a lot of cash around with you, even stay at hotels without having to leave a deposit or prepay. About the only differences with debit cards right now is that many rental car companies won't accept them, and you have to have the money in your account at the time of purchase.

Generally, you won't need a credit check to get a debit card. However, if you bounced more than two checks in the past year, you may need to get special permission to have a debit card.

One way to avoid bounced checks is to see if your bank offers a "savings sweep" where they automatically move money from your savings to your checking to cover checks that come in.

How Exactly Do Debit Cards Work?

As far as the merchant is concerned, a debit card looks and acts just like a credit card, when you go to buy something. The main way credit cards and debit cards differ is how you actually pay for your purchases.

With a credit card, a merchant checks to see if you have enough credit available on your card to buy what you want to buy. Then they charge that purchase amount to your credit card account and bill you at the end of each month. You then pay for all your purchases and bring your debt back down to zero, or you pay for part of your purchases and carry the balance — and a finance charge — onto your next month's statement.

With a debit card, however, a merchant checks to see if you have enough available on your card to buy what you want to buy. But, instead of the computer checking on your available credit line, the computer checks to see how much money is available in your checking account.

The money is then subtracted from your checking account immediately or within three business days, just as if you had paid for it by check. Your card's limit is your checking account balance.

But remember: the amount the bank says you have and the amount you really have available to "charge" against, will be different if you wrote checks that haven't cleared your account yet, or if you've taken money out of your account with an ATM card. On the plus side, you don't pay any finance charges with a debit card.

The Downside to Debit Cards

Debit cards are a great tool to use when you're worried about running up debt again. However, a debit card *will not* help you rebuild your credit. In most cases, you'll need to have at least one credit card listed on your credit report to rebuild your credit to the point where creditors will be willing to offer you a mortgage or car loan in the future.

You can safely use a good secured credit card to rebuild your credit, along with your debit card if you like. Get the secured card and always pay it off every month. Charge only the items that you would normally buy that month with cash. And immediately pay for the item that you've charged.

For example, say you're getting a gift for someone and you planned on spending $50. Take your $50 check and send it to the credit card company as a payment the same day that you buy the item using the charge card. Write out the check to the credit card company in the exact amount you paid for the item, just like you were paying for it with a check. This way, you never have to worry about buying things on the credit card that you can't afford right now — while you're rebuilding your credit.

If you decide you want to use a debit card in addition to a secured credit card, make sure you can answer these questions:

1. *Does the debit card report my payment history to the credit bureaus?* Most debit cards don't report your payment history to the credit bureaus. You're not rebuilding your credit history because the money is automatically taken out of your checking account, like an ATM card that's used to buy things at the Point of Service (P.O.S.).

If you want the convenience of using plastic and the security of using cash from your checking account rather than going into debt with a credit card, then using a debit card won't cause a problem. But, if you're trying to rebuild your credit, a debit card won't help.

2. *What protection do I have if my debit card is stolen?* With a credit card, even a secured credit card, you're usually only responsible for the first $50 charged to your card when it's been reported stolen. But, with a debit card, you may not have the same protection. Be sure to ask — and make sure you're comfortable with the answer you get — before you get a debit card.

3. *What protection do I have if I go "over my limit" with my debit card?* Like an ATM card, the balance listed on your debit card may differ from the money you actually have available in your checking account. You may have written checks on your account that haven't yet cleared your bank and the available balance on your debit card could be more than is in your checking account, if you take these checks into account. Which means you could run the risk of bouncing checks.

That's one reason why I only recommend debit cards if you're really good at balancing your checkbook and always know how much is available in your account. Otherwise, bounced check fees could eat you alive. One protection against this, of course, is if your bank offers an automatic "savings sweep" where money from your savings account is automatically moved into your checking account (for a small fee of around $2 a transaction) to cover any checks or debits that exceed the balance in your checking account.

4. *Will my debit card protect me if I have a dispute with a merchant I bought something from?* Be sure you read the fine print on the application — with a "credit" card your credit card issuer will dispute any merchandise problem for you. This is a "chargeback right." But not all debit cards offer this protection.

For example, *Fleet Bank*, in particular, clearly states that "You give up all merchant dispute rights." *First Chicago*, however, is a bank that has gone out of its way to help consumers who have a problem with something they bought on their debit card. Make sure you read the fine print if you're interested in getting a particular debit card, and don't sign anything until you get answers to these five questions:

1. *Is there any monthly or annual fee, and if so, how much is it?*

2. *How much will I be charged for using the card at another bank's ATM?*

3. *How much will I be charged every time I buy something, either as a VISA purchase or as a Point-Of-Service, ATM purchase?* Many times, you won't be charged anything to use your debit card as a VISA but you will be charged if you buy something with your debit card as an ATM transaction. When in doubt, use your debit card as a VISA.

4. *What are my daily limits for charging or withdrawing cash with my debit card?* (This is VERY important, especially if

you want to use your card when you're traveling.) Most banks limit the amount you can withdraw each day using your debit card as an ATM card, usually to around $300 a day. But, if you use your debit card as a VISA, you can often charge as much as you have available in your account.

5. When will deposits be credited to my account for my debit card — and when will charges be subtracted?

If you get a debit card, save all your receipts and check them against your bank statements. Also, remember to subtract the transaction, and any fees, directly from your checkbook on the day you use your debit card. This will help you avoid bouncing checks.

Now, let's talk about how to control your credit card bills.

Three Tips For Keeping Your Credit Card Bills Under Control

Controlling your credit card spending is going to be easier than you think. I had really bad spending habits before I declared bankruptcy — my credit cards were always maxed out — but I managed to stay out of debt after my bankruptcy by getting a secured credit card with a $500 limit. Then I followed these tips:

• *Only charge what you can pay off this month.* You don't need a giant credit line to get by. Start yourself off with a $200-$500 limit to test out what you can afford. You can't fall into enormous debt with a $500 credit limit. And you can usually pay off this amount in a few months in a pinch. If you find that one month you can't completely pay off your bill, do yourself an enormous favor and stick your credit card in the freezer in a plastic bag filled with water and don't use it for ANYTHING until you get the bill paid off in full!

• *Pay off your credit card bill as soon it arrives.* This is one credit reference you don't ever want to show up late on your credit report — don't risk misplacing the bill. Pay it right away.

• *Prepay your credit card bill.* Every holiday season, or before a vacation, I always send in an extra few hundred dollars so the money I spend has already been credited to my charge card — keeping me out of debt.

Using these strategies, you'll find that you can stay out of debt almost effortlessly.

Getting a Gasoline Credit Card

Here's a strategy you can use to get a gas station credit card after you've declared bankruptcy. This strategy is similar to the one you use to get a secured credit card — except your money will be invested in *stock* instead of in a bank savings account. This lets you get a credit card and become a stock investor at the same time.

The secret is to choose a gas company that has stations near where you live and work — and to choose a company that is a sound investment. I recommend buying shares from companies that let you buy your stock directly through their direct purchase and dividend reinvestment programs (DRIPs). This way you bypass the broker's commission (usually saving yourself $25-$50).

Two major companies offer direct purchase of their stock: *ExxonMobil* and *Texaco*. You must buy at least $250 worth of stock in order to enroll in each company's DRIP. In essence, you'll be securing your credit card with your stock certificate. Once you decide which company will give you the best deal (the safest stock and the most nearby locations for gas), you can buy your stock from the company and in a few months they'll send you an application for a gas credit card.

For the first year or so that you have the gas credit card, you'll have to pay off your balance in full each month, which will help you keep from adding more debt than you can pay off each month. Eventually, the gas company will let you carry a balance from month to month. If you do wind up carrying a balance on your gas card, I recommend putting the credit card away until you get the balance paid off — these gas company cards usually charge 21% (or higher) interest, which will eat you alive.

Another thing to beware: Gasoline companies have turned their bills into mini mail order catalogs with high priced merchandise that you can pay for in "installments." But the company posts the entire balance due on your bill and you pay interest each month on the outstanding balance.

Some "installment!" And this is on top of the high price of the merchandise. Save your money. If you see an item you "must have," shop around — chances are other catalogs or warehouse stores will have the item you're looking for, at a much lower cost.

Checking The Safety Of A Gas Company's Stock

When you're selecting a gasoline company, there are a few basic criteria you should look at to measure the stock's safety and its growth potential. This way you can tilt the odds of finding a strong company in your favor.

1. *Is the company an industry leader or does it have the potential to be a leader?*

2. *Does the company have consistently increasing sales and profits?*

3. *Does the company have 30% or less of its capital tied up in debt?*

4. *Has the company had an annual return of 10% or more for the past 5 years?*

Two gasoline companies meet these stringent criteria and offer DRIPs. For each company you want a credit card from, you'll need to make an initial investment (deposit) of $250.

• *ExxonMobil* (NYSE:XOM). c/o EquiServe Trust Company, NA, *ExxonMobil* Shareholder Services, Box 8033, Boston, MA 02266-8033; 800/252-1800. $50 minimum subsequent investment.

• *Texaco, Inc.* (NYSE:TX). 2000 Westchester Ave., White Plains, NY 10650; 800/283-9785, Shareholder Relations; 914/253-6084, Administrator. $50 minimum subsequent investment.

With *ExxonMobil,* you can even have your money invested inside an IRA account — just check off the box for "IRA investment" on the investment form. The advantages: the money you invest grows tax-deferred and you may even get a tax deduction for your IRA contributions.

How To Start Investing Your Money So It Keeps On Growing

When you're ready to get a gasoline credit card, call the toll-free number listed above for the company you're interested in. Tell the representative that *you want to join their dividend reinvestment plan.* Don't say you want to apply for a credit card. (You'll wind up getting transferred to the credit card division if you do, and then you'll get turned down when you apply.)

In a few days, you'll receive an information packet with details on how to purchase shares of stock directly from the company.

I bought my stock from *Texaco.* The company met all the criteria for a solid growth stock, it was paying a yield of over 6%, and there were several *Texaco's* near my house. When I got my information packet, I filled out the form showing how I wanted my name listed as a stockholder and sent it back with my $250 "deposit" investment. The company then enrolled me in their DRIP and bought me $250 worth of *Texaco* stock.

Each time *Texaco* declares a dividend, they post this amount to my account, the same way your bank posts interest on your savings account statement. Only with a DRIP, the company essentially uses your dividend payment to buy you more shares of the company's stock — so you own even more stock.

Four to six months after I enrolled in *Texaco's* DRIP, I received a credit card application extending an invitation for me to apply for a *Texaco* gas card. I filled out the application and sent it back in. My credit card arrived in the mail six weeks later.

One reader who put this advice to work found it to be very profitable. He started out by opening a dividend reinvestment account with *Exxon* before its merger with Mobil.

Within 6 months, he received a pre-approved credit card application and he had been using his credit card for several months before he wrote me to share his success.

He not only made the initial $250 investment with *Exxon*, but he also dollar-cost averages into *Exxon*, buying shares each month.

In his own words, this has proven to be a very good investment! When he made his first investment, *Exxon* shares were trading at $82 a share.

When he wrote to me, *Exxon* shares were up to $100, and he was reinvesting the dividends too, which as he said, are quite generous.

Take advantage of this opportunity to improve your credit and start building an investment portfolio with gasoline stocks. You'll be glad you did.

Anytime you want, you can add more money to your DRIP account — and continue to build your stock holdings. There's no easier way to safely enter the stock market — and rebuild your credit.

TOP SECURED CREDIT CARDS

Bank	Min./Max. Deposit	Interest Rate	Yield on Savings	Net Interest	Annual Fee	Cash Adv. Fee	Other Fees
American Pacific Bank 800/610-1201	$300-$15,000 (Pers.); $1,000-$15,000 (Bus.)	17.40%	2.50%	14.90%	$35 (Pers.) $45 (Bus.)	3% of advance ($5 minimum)	Late Payment ($25) Over-Limit ($25) Bounced Check ($25)
Capital One 800/548-4593	$99-$1,000	19.80%	2.59%	17.21%	$39	2.5% of advance ($2.50 minimum)	Late Payment ($25) Over-Limit ($25) Bounced Check ($25)
First Consumers National Bank 800/876-3262	$100-$2,500	19.90%	2.00%	17.90%	$39	2.5% of advance ($2.50 minimum)	Late Payment ($20) Over-Limit ($20) Bounced Check ($20)
First Premier Bank 800/987-5521	$200-$10,000	18.90% <$1,000; 16.9% over	NONE	16.90%-18.9%	$45	2% of advance ($2 minimum)	Late Payment ($20) Over-Limit ($20) Bounced Check ($20)
First Union 800/413-7914	$400-$15,000	18.90% (9.9% + prime)	1.49%	17.41%	$35	3% of advance ($3 minimum)	Late Payment ($25) Over-Limit ($25) Bounced Check ($25)
Metropolitan Credit Union 800/225-5908	$500-$10,000	13.90%	2.55%	11.35%	$45	$0.95/trans.	Late Payment ($10) Over-Limit ($10) Bounced Check ($20)

Chapter 4: Action Items

1. Review the different terms you need to know to shop for the best secured credit card.

2. Decide what's most important to you in a secured credit card: a low interest rate, a high yield on your security deposit, a low annual fee, etc.

3. Double check to make sure the credit card you want reports your payment history but *doesn't* report the card as secured.

4. Call 2-3 different secured cards from this list and get applications from each to help you decide which one you want to apply for.

5. Fill out and send in your application, along with your security deposit check.

6. Write Equifax and request to be taken off the mailing list for future credit card offers.

7. Decide if a debit card would be a better option for most of the purchases you'll be "charging."

8. Examine your debit card application carefully to make sure it's a good debit card.

9. Apply for a "secured" gasoline credit card and start investing in your financial future.

chapter 5

Ready To Buy A New Set Of Wheels?

When you're ready to buy a new car, here are a few strategies you can use to buy your car without credit — plus a few strategies that will help you get a car loan. Once again, I know these techniques work because I've used them myself or have seen others use them successfully.

Need A Car Before Your Credit Report Is Completely Cleaned Up or While You're Still in Chapter 13?

If you need a car before your credit report is completely cleaned up, or if you're still making payments on your Chapter 13 bankruptcy you'll probably have to pay cash for your new car. I'm not talking about doling out tens of thousands of dollars. I'm talking about shopping around for a reasonably-priced, reliable car. Shop the classifieds, college billboards, places like that. Pay particular attention to ads that say "ugly but reliable."

If you're still making payments under your Chapter 13 bankruptcy, you will need to get the trustee's permission before you buy a car. Chances are good, however, that the trustee will work with you to fit the car into your budget.

Start small. You should be able to buy a decent car for $500-$1,000, but be sure to have any car inspected by a *trusted* mechanic before you buy it.

When I declared bankruptcy, my car had been sold at auction after being impounded for unpaid parking tickets. My car loan was listed on my bankruptcy, which made it virtually impossible for me to get a car loan right after my bankruptcy.

Instead, I bought a 1982 Honda Civic hatchback. This car had been in two fender benders, was rusty but reliable, and cost me $200. The owner was selling it because she lived in the city, had just bought a new BMW and didn't have room to park two cars.

I drove that Civic for five years and put a total of $1,000 into it for a new clutch, muffler and brakes. I never had a car payment though — and I used that extra money to pay off debts that weren't included in my bankruptcy.

Grand total, I spent $1,200 on my car over five years. I then sold the car in 1991 to a college student for $500 (150% more than what I paid for the car). My total cost came to $700 — or $140 a year.

I then bought a 1980 Toyota Corona for $250 and pocketed the extra $250. Two years later, however, I needed a car that I could drive clients around in for my employer. By this time, I'd carefully rebuilt my credit. I had been using a secured credit card for five years. I had a gasoline credit card from *Texaco*. Now I could apply for a car loan.

Ready To Get A Car Loan?

Before I approached a bank for a car loan, I needed to figure out which car I wanted. A late model car with low repairs was a must. And I knew I didn't want to buy a brand new car

because the value depreciates the minute you drive off the lot —
and I didn't want to get saddled with a car loan that went on for
years and years. I decided to stick with a car that I could comfortably pay off in two years. That meant I could afford a $6,000 car
loan.

Looking through *Consumers Reports*, I narrowed my
choices down to two cars — a 1988 Honda Accord LXi, and a
1988 Toyota Corolla. The local classifieds showed that these cars
were selling for about $7,000.

Next, I got the word out that I was looking for these two
cars. I told all my friends, neighbors, family members and co-
workers. And I told them to tell all their friends, neighbors,
family members and coworkers. Within a few weeks someone got
back to me about a doctor who was thinking of selling his car — a
1988 Honda Accord LXi Coupe. I really had my heart set on a 4-
door sedan, but I went to look at the car. It was garage-kept, had
been well-maintained and only had 40,000 miles on it. He
wanted $7,000 — about $150 less than the blue book value.

So, I went to see my banker. That's when the real fun
started. When I applied for my car loan, I was completely up-
front with the loan officer about my past bankruptcy. Everything
was going smoothly until the loan officer got my credit report,
which showed an unpaid lien from a landlord I'd had — five years
before. I had no idea that a judgment had been made against me.
So I also had no idea that this negative information was on my
credit report.

I had to call the landlord's attorney to find out how much
I owed ($93). Then I had to go pay this money and get a receipt.
Then I had to take the receipt to the courthouse to prove the lien
had been satisfied. The courthouse gave me a certificate of

release, which I took to my loan officer, and finally I got my car loan.

Also, that student loan with the computer glitch showed up on my credit report. Needless to say, the loan officer was ready to turn down my loan, based on the information in my credit report.

When I finally requested my credit report, I saw what my creditors had been seeing: really bad debts — even though I had been diligently making payments after declaring bankruptcy. Was I ever miffed!

I finally got a letter from the student loan lender stating that my student loan account was current and that the problem was a computer error. But I could have lost my shot at the car if the seller hadn't been a "friend of a friend." Which is why I recommend making sure you know what's on your credit report *before* you talk to any potential lender. And the very best lender to start with is your banker, *not* the dealer's finance department.

When you see your banker, be very up-front about your bankruptcy. Show your banker how you've worked to rebuild your credit. Your bankruptcy will not matter to the banker, once it's two years old. What will matter most to the banker is your most recent payment history for the last year or so. As long as you've taken steps to rebuild your credit after your bankruptcy, you'll be in a good position to get a decent interest rate on your car loan.

Ask your banker for a three-year car loan for 90% of the car's cost. Chances are you'll get a loan for 80%, and that it will be a two-year loan, but it's worth trying for the best loan possible.

With a two-year loan, your banker is hedging her bet. If you default on the loan, the car will still be worth enough for the bank to recoup its expenses. So don't be offended if your banker isn't willing to go out on a limb to help you get a loan. The banking industry is in pretty bad shape these days and they're being stingy with loans.

You can sometimes sway your banker by opening up a 30-day Certificate of Deposit (CD) for $500 or so. Opening a CD is also a nice gesture to thank your banker when you finally get your car loan — especially if you wind up getting your loan from a bank that you don't normally do business with, as I did. I got a $6,000 loan and paid the seller $1,000 in cash to close the deal.

Should You Get a Co-Signer?

You may find that you need to finance a car loan before lenders are ready to give you one on your own. I'm still a big advocate for paying cash for a car you *can* afford before taking on new debt right after your bankruptcy is discharged. But sometimes that's not practical, especially if your job requires you to travel a lot and you need a very reliable car.

If you need to, use a co-signer. After your bankruptcy has been discharged for at least two years, you should take steps to get a car loan in your name alone, without a co-signer. Sit down with the lender who holds the note on the current car you have (or the dealer who arranged the financing for you). Bring with you a notarized letter from your co-signer, stating that you've been the one making the payments since the beginning of the note, and that your payments have always been on time.

Explain to the lender that you'd like to trade in the current car, and get a different car, and that you're looking for financing. Ask, *"What amount would you qualify me for?"* Chances are, you can get a good deal on a car loan, for 80% of the car's value, with a repayment period of 2-3 years.

Make sure the car you buy fits into your budget and that you could comfortably repay that amount during that period of time. If you know exactly how much you can afford to pay toward the car loan each month, ask, *"How much could I borrow to make sure I'm not paying more than $xxx a month?"*

The Best Way to Buy a Car From A Dealer

If you do buy your car from a dealer, keep the focus on how much you want to pay for the car, *not* on how much you can afford to pay each month. For example, tell a dealer that you're looking to buy a car that's two to three years old and that you want to spend no more than $7,000 on the car. The dealer wants you to commit to as large a monthly payment as you can afford, in order to get the most interest out of you they can.

Instead of putting the dealer in charge of your finances, put yourself in charge. Start by calculating how much car you can afford to pay off in two years. If you can afford to spend $250 a month on a car payment, then you can afford to finance $6,000 over two years. You don't want to tell the dealer you can spend $250 a month because the dealer will want to hook you up with a $250 payment for 48 months, financing $12,000 instead of $6,000.

A good dealer will work with you to buy the amount of car you want to buy. A good dealer will stop trying to sell you on the "low monthly payment" as soon as they see that you are serious about wanting to spend no more than the price you've determined. Put down as much as you can afford to put down toward the total price of the car. This will help you get a better deal on the interest rate, but as you'll see in a minute, the interest rate you're charged isn't as important as the fact that you're about to get another piece of good credit on your credit report.

Once you pay off any bills that weren't discharged in your bankruptcy, and you've driven around in your reliable clunker for a year, putting aside money toward your down payment, you're ready to go out and get that $7,000 car. Go to the dealer and pick out the car you want, preferably a two- to three-year old car.

Take your time deciding what car you want, and be flexible. My former spouse and I wandered around for over a year using just one car, getting up early to arrange car schedules — which wasn't always easy, given that we were located 20-45 minutes from *everything*. The right car will appear while you're saving the money to pay for it.

We decided to put down on paper the specifics of what we needed in a car, and we were flexible with any other options that happened to be included. My criteria were: 4-door sedan, cruise control, tilt steering wheel, AM-FM cassette stereo and power windows. Of course, I'd have loved for the car to have a leather interior, sunroof, power locks and a CD player. But I put down the basics so others would know what type of car I wanted.

I wanted a 4-door car so it would be easy to get a car seat in and out. I wanted cruise control so my leg wouldn't fall asleep when I'm driving long distances. I wanted a tilt steering wheel to make it easier for a pregnant lady to get behind the wheel. I wanted a cassette player, so I could listen to my favorite books on tape and motivational tapes. And finally, I wanted power windows so I didn't have to break my arm at the toll plazas.

What criteria are important to you? Put them down on a piece of paper where you can look at them throughout the day (your bathroom mirror is a great location). And tell everyone you know what you're looking for in a car, so they'll keep you in mind when they come across cars for sale that meet your criteria.

Once you know what you want in a car, check out the blue book trade in and dealer prices for different cars that fit your criteria. Your local library will probably have reference books that will give you the information you're looking for. Also, you can go on-line to either http://www.kbb.com (Kellys Blue Book values) or http://www.edmunds.com (Edmunds car values). Both sites break down costs for various cars. Let your fingers do the walking until you've narrowed down your search to several cars in the price range you want, and that meet the criteria you have set. Then check each car's reliability using *Consumer Reports*.

Once you've done your homework, you're ready to actually buy your car. Go see the dealer, remembering to tell him or her how much you want to spend for the car. In our example, we're using $7,000 as our target price. Put down as large a deposit as you can afford. The more you can put down, the better your interest rate will be — and the lower your monthly payment will be.

After you've agreed upon a car and a price, tell the dealer how much you can put down and that you want to finance the balance. If you can put down $3,000, finance the remaining $4,000. But don't finance the loan over two years. Instead, ask to have a 48-month loan so your car payment is around $100. While you might be able to afford a higher car payment, the trick is to not get yourself trapped into paying a higher monthly payment. Instead, go ahead and pay $250 a month toward your car if you want. You'll have the $4,000 loan paid off in 16 months if you do. Or pay $175 a month and pay off the car in two years.

Your financial situation could change in an instant, and I don't want you saddled with a huge debt burden. Instead, use that extra money each month to build up your savings and to buy some of the items you want that you used to charge each month. Above all else, promise me that you won't do business with "Bad Credit, No Problem" dealers. These dealers will sell you an overpriced car and stick you with a high-interest car loan.

If you qualify for a loan at the interest rates they charge, chances are very good that you can get a car loan on your own — with a low interest rate. Don't let any dealer bully you into thinking that you automatically have to pay a higher interest rate. It just ain't so!

Finally, when you're ready to insure your car, make sure you take out collision insurance until your car loan is paid off. This way, if anything happens to your car — like it gets totaled — you aren't stuck paying a car loan on a car that is a pile of junkyard tin.

Keep the deductible as high as you can afford and your insurance premiums will be cheaper. I started out with a $100 deductible. Once I had saved $250, I raised the deductible to $250, then $500 and so on until my deductible was $1,000. I paid off my two year car loan early in 1995 and used my $239 monthly payment to increase my savings so I could raise my deductible.

If you have to, create a completely separate savings account specifically for your insurance deductibles. This way, you'll never have to worry about where the money will come from to meet your deductible.

What If You Already Have a High-Interest Car Loan

You're not alone if you have already gotten a new car after bankruptcy — at a high interest rate. I talked with a man on-line once who had gotten a car loan with a 24% interest rate! If this has happened to you, there may be a way for you to get out from under this high interest rate.

First, if your car is less than two years old, you might have some luck refinancing the loan at a lower interest rate. Start by going to your bank, or several area banks, and seeing if they offer refinancing for recently purchased cars.

If you can't find a bank that will lower your interest, then go back to the original lender. Don't settle for talking to someone at the front of the office.

Ask to speak to someone in authority, or, if you prefer, write a letter to the president of the company, explaining that you would like them to lower the interest rate or you will have to sell the car.

Use the sample letter on the next page to get you started.

(Date)

[President's Name]
[Name of Lender]
[Address]
[City, Sate, Zip Code]

　　RE: [Your automobile loan number]

Dear [President's Name]:

　　On [date you purchased your car] I obtained a car loan from you to finance the purchase of a [type of car, year, make and model]. The interest rate which I was given was [percentage interest rate], which is outrageously high. This interest rate is so high, in fact, that I am faced with a dilemma:

　　Either I convince you to reduce the interest rate to a more reasonable rate of [indicate the rate you'd be willing to pay] or I will be forced to sell my car.

　　I would like to continue my relationship with your company, but I cannot continue to pay this outrageously high interest rate. I look forward to hearing from you in the next 30 days to see if we can get this interest rate lowered to [the rate you listed above].

　　　　Sincerely,
　　　　[Your Name]

With this letter, you put the ball in the lender's court. They will most likely make you a counteroffer of an interest rate somewhere in the middle of what you're asking for. If your current interest rate is 24%, and the going interest rate is 10%, ask for a 13% interest rate in your letter. When the lender counteroffers, decide how high you really want to go with the interest rate.

The lender has three choices: Try and get as much interest as they think they can get from you; go with the 13% you asked for; or risk getting nothing from you because you've sold the car to get out from under their high interest rate. Send your letter certified, return receipt requested and keep a copy for your files.

Leasing a Car —
Don't, Unless You Have No Other Choice

Leasing deals might look good at first glance, but the fine print can really sink you. I strongly recommend against leasing unless you're a business owner and there's an incredible tax advantage to leasing through your company. With a lease, your monthly payments may be quite attractive, but at the end of the lease you'll have paid out a great deal of money without actually having bought anything. If you do decide to lease, make sure you get a closed-end lease where you can walk away from the car once the lease expires.

When you lease, you need to find out how much the dealer cost is on the car you want to lease and how much the residual value is for a 2-year old or 4-year old version of that same make and model. These figures will let you calculate whether or not you're being charged a fair amount over the life of your lease. By subtracting the residual cost from the dealer cost, you'll know how much you should be paying over the life of your lease.

You can get the dealer cost from *Consumer Reports*, by sending the make, model and exact style of the car you want, plus a check or money order for $12 (and $10 for any additional cars requested) to *Consumer Reports*, P.O. Box 8005, Novi, MI 48376; 800/234-1645. You can get the residual value (the "Blue Book value") of the make, model and exact style of the car you want at the library or on-line. If you want a two-year lease, get the residual value on a 2-year old car. If you want a three-year lease, get the residual value on a 3-year old car.

For example, say you want a two year lease on a Toyota Camry. Let's say the current dealer cost for the Camry is $30,000 and the current value, or residual cost, for a two-year old Camry is $24,000. To make sure you're not overpaying on your lease, the total sum of your lease payment *and* any down payment you make shouldn't exceed $6,000 ($30,000- $24,000).

If you're being offered a "no-money down" two-year lease, then your monthly payments should be no more than $250 per month ($6,000/24 months). If you make a standard down payment of $1,250, then you would subtract that amount from the $6,000 *before* dividing it by 24 payments. In this case, your monthly lease payments shouldn't exceed $4,750, or $197.92 per month ($4,750/24 months).

Do the math for a three year and a four year lease as well, before you see the dealer, so you're not trying to compare apples to oranges. For a four year lease, let's say that the residual cost on a four-year old Camry is $19,000. In this case, your total lease payments shouldn't exceed $11,000 ($30,000 - $19,000). Divided by 48 months, your monthly payments in this example would be $229.17 or less.

The biggest mistake people make when they lease is trying to drive more car than they can actually afford. If that's your main reason for leasing, I urge you to reconsider and buy a car instead. You might not be able to get the car of your dreams right now, but you'll be able to get a car that will keep you rebuilding your financial security.

Remember to stick with a car you can afford. Once all your debts are paid off, you can turn your sights on that sportster. For now though, stick with an affordable car that will get you where you need to be going. You'll get richer a whole lot faster if you rebuild your finances without the extra stress and strain of high car loan payments.

Chapter 5: Action Items

1. Pay cash for your next car, if possible, even if it means getting an "ugly but reliable" car.

2. Get copies of your credit reports *before* you go see a car lender about getting a car loan.

3. Get a co-signer if you need to get a better car right after bankruptcy — then convert the car loan to your name or trade in the car after two years have passed.

4. Concentrate on the bottom line of how much *total* you can afford to spend on a car, rather than on the *monthly payment amount*.

5. Negotiate with your car lender if you already have a high interest rate car loan.

6. If you must lease, calculate the cost of leasing *before* you go see the dealer.

chapter 6

Easing Your Job Fears After Bankruptcy

By law, your employer can't fire you or discriminate against you solely because you filed bankruptcy. In addition, if you're applying for a job with the government, you can't be turned down for the job simply because you went bankrupt.

Can You Lose Your Job?

Your employer will probably never find out that you've declared bankruptcy. And if your employer does find out, either because you need a security clearance or your employer needs to run a credit check, your employer will probably support your decision to declare bankruptcy.

That's because once you declare bankruptcy, your mind goes back to getting your job done. In addition, declaring bankruptcy puts an end to collection calls at the office, and your employer won't have to set up and enforce garnishment of your wages, if your state allows garnishment.

Your employer may have to put up with a few inconveniences when you declare bankruptcy, including payroll deductions for Chapter 13 payments, allowing you time off for court appearances, as well as attendance at budgeting and personal finance courses, which are usually all held during business hours.

Even so, your employer cannot change your employment status just because of your bankruptcy. An employer who tries to demote you or fire you because you need time off to attend court appearances or classes would be in violation of the anti-discrimination provisions of the bankruptcy code. In addition, discrimination against any employee for bankruptcy is expressly prohibited by Section 525 of the bankruptcy code.

Most employers will support your decision to file bankruptcy, because it represents a first step toward overcoming your financial distress. In fact, some employers are actually paying the attorney fees for their employees, to get their employees' minds back on their jobs. One woman I met on-line has been at her job for only a year and half. She had this wonderful experience to share about her boss' reaction to her bankruptcy:

> *My boss is actually helping me through the bankruptcy process. Another manager in my office told him of my inability to buy groceries and do laundry due to the high volume of bills I have. He immediately called me into his office, sat me down and proceeded to explain what declaring bankruptcy would do for my situation (risks and benefits).*

> *He stated that my emotional and physical well being was at stake. He also knows full well that these factors have a profound impact on job performance. He even went so far as to call prominent attorneys in this area looking for references and made an appointment for me.*

If you feel that you're being discriminated against, however, or have been fired because of your bankruptcy, I recommend that you contact a debtors' rights or employment attorney immediately.

Finding a New Job With a Credit Check

Nowadays, when you apply for a job, chances are good that your potential employer will check your credit report as well as your references. Luckily, having a bankruptcy on your credit report will hurt your chances of landing a job *less* than having poor credit, or a history of poor credit.

There's no evidence that a good credit report is an indicator of good job performance. And in most cases, you'll only need to worry about what your credit report says if the job you're applying for requires handling large amounts of money, or if you're going to be in a sensitive position. That's because people with huge amounts of debt are considered more susceptible to blackmail, bribery or theft. But again, a bankruptcy makes you *less* susceptible, because you've now gotten rid of your debts.

Bottom line: One bankruptcy will not disqualify you as a candidate at most companies. However, having a number of credit problems, or lots of late payments or canceled credit cards *could* disqualify you — which is why employers look a bit more favorably on a bankruptcy than active, but poor, credit accounts.

To an employer, a good credit report tends to indicate that you have a sense of responsibility and an ability to plan. More and more employers are doing credit checks these days and they sometimes use credit reports as a tie breaker. You'll have advance notice that the employer is looking at your credit report because, by law, they can't pull your credit report unless you've signed a release giving them permission to do so. If you think a job comes down to you and one other person, I recommend being up-front about your past bankruptcy.

The employer will appreciate your honesty and will take that into consideration when looking at your credit report. Rehearse your statement about why you declared bankruptcy and what you've done since to get yourself back on your feet again.

Put yourself in the employer's shoes for a minute. The biggest concern an employer has is this: *"Will this person represent my company well and not take advantage of me or mismanage my company's money?"*

If you are rejected for a job based on an item in your credit report, the company must give you a copy of the report before they turn you down. You can then check over the information to make sure that what they're seeing is correct.

The fact is, you can't control how future employers might view your credit rating. So I encourage you to concentrate on what you *can* control, which is putting your bankruptcy and your past credit problems behind you. Future employers will be very grateful to see that you've dealt with these problems, since now your mind will be focused on doing your job, and not on fending off bill collectors!

Chapter 6: Action Items

1. Be up-front with your employer about your bankruptcy, whenever possible.

2. Use your bankruptcy as a strength when talking with future employers.

3. Concentrate on putting your bankruptcy behind you and doing the best job possible!

chapter 7

Rent The Apartment Or House You Want After Bankruptcy

Are you currently renting an apartment or home?

Chances are good that your current landlord will never know that you declared bankruptcy, as long as you didn't list your landlord in your bankruptcy.

However, if you're looking to relocate and need to rent a home or apartment again, you can, even if you did list your current landlord in your bankruptcy.

In this chapter, I'll walk you through, step-by-step, the strategies to take to make sure that you get the apartment or house you want.

Strategies to Get the Rental You Want

Your best bet when you're ready to rent a new apartment or house is to find one that is for rent through a private landlord. Your local classified ads will offer your best opportunity for finding people who want to rent out individual rental properties.

You can also ask friends who live in apartments for the name of the owner of their building. That way, you have a good chance of approaching the owner directly.

Since most apartment complexes now ask in their applications, "have you ever declared bankruptcy" I recommend being open and honest about it. They're going to see your bankruptcy listed on your credit report when they request a copy, so there's no reason to try and hide it.

What are they looking for when they request your credit report? They're looking for derogatory accounts — accounts that are past due or have been chronically paid late. This gives them a good indication of whether or not you're likely to pay your rent on time.

Many people who are turned down for apartments after declaring bankruptcy haven't looked at their credit reports or updated them the way you have (Chapter 1) to make sure that the accounts that were discharged under the bankruptcy are being correctly reported.

Most major apartment complexes have strict rules and won't rent an apartment to anyone who has more than two bad accounts on their credit report. Once your bankruptcy is discharged, you can start to counteract the negative account information in three ways:

1. *Updating your accounts to show they were discharged under your bankruptcy;*

2. *Getting a secured credit card; and*

3. *Getting a letter from your current landlord showing that you are current on your payments.*

Talking With the Landlord

When you go in person to apply for an apartment, come equipped with your own personal credit references.

Bring a copy of your credit report, a recent paystub, reference letters from your employer, your current landlord, etc., and a one or two paragraph explanation of why you declared bankruptcy and what steps you've taken since then to start rebuilding your credit. Don't make excuses, just state the simple facts.

Landlords are looking for reliable tenants who will pay their rent on time and will respect their property. Offer to pay an extra month's security deposit as a good faith gesture. This will often help you win your case.

Chapter 7: Action Items

1. Search out private landlords whenever possible.

2. Update your credit reports before looking for a new place to rent.

3. Get a secured credit card for a positive credit reference.

4. Get references from your current landlord.

5. Offer to pay an extra month's security deposit.

chapter 8

How To Travel Without Credit

Believe it or not, traveling without credit is actually very easy. Hotels, motels and car rental agencies all offer "credit-less" options. Most hotels and airlines will also accept debit cards, but more and more rental car agencies won't accept debit cards. The key to traveling without credit, in most cases, is to plan ahead. Make your reservations 10-30 days before you travel and you're guaranteed to be able to travel without a credit card.

How To Reserve A Hotel Room Without A Credit Card

Nowadays, most hotels and motels expect you to guarantee your reservations with a credit or debit card, but most hotels also have policies regarding "credit-less" travel that let you get around this requirement. In general, you prepay for your entire stay or simply prepay your deposit (usually one night's cost).

The best part of prepaying is that you can then travel without carrying a lot of cash. If you don't prepay, I strongly recommend picking up Travelers Cheques at your bank or local AAA office — I don't want a lost or stolen wallet to ruin your trip.

To find out a particular chain's policy, call the hotel's toll free 800 number. (You can get this number from directory assistance — 800/555-1212). Ask about the hotel's "credit-less" policy. Some hotels have company-wide policies; others decide their policies hotel-by-hotel. Here are the policies at the major chains:

Best Western (800/528-1238)

Best Western has a Centralized Prepayment Program that lets you prepay a cash deposit for one night's stay, at any Best Western location, at least 14 days before your intended stay. When you arrive at the Best Western where you are planning to stay, you then pay any taxes owed for that night's stay. Depending on the individual hotel, you can then pay for the rest of your stay with a personal check or company check. Call the hotel you're planning on staying at for their policy.

Choice Hotels International (800/221-2222)

These hotels include: Choice Hotels, Quality Inn, Comfort Inn, Sleep Inn, Rodeway Inn, Econolodge and Friendship Inn. At Choice, individual hotels make their own policies regarding "credit-less" travel. If you're using a money order, you can pay your room deposit as late as the day before you arrive. If you're paying with a personal check, you need to pay 10 days before you arrive. You can go to any hotel in the chain to pay the deposit for your first night's stay. The hotel will even give you a voucher that you can take with you if you'll be checking in late.

Hilton (800/445-8667)

You can reserve a room at Hilton and use a company or personal check to pay for your first night's deposit. Your check must be received within seven days after you make your reservation. At some locations you can also arrange to prepay your entire stay. Call the location where you'll be staying and ask the hotel's credit manager for their specific policy.

Holiday Inn (800/465-4329)

You can pay a deposit for your first night's stay as long as your payment is received at least two days before you arrive. You can pay with a money order or a company check. If you're traveling on business, you can also guarantee your room with your company's Holiday Inn corporate account number. Call for more information on Holiday Inn's policies.

Hyatt (800/233-1234)

At some Hyatt hotels, you can guarantee your room by paying a deposit for the first night. You can pay your deposit with either a company check or a personal check. Or, if you stay at a Hyatt at least once a year, you can join Hyatt's Gold Passport program and guarantee your reservations without a credit card OR a deposit! To enroll in the program, call 800/544-9288.

Marriott (800/228-9290)

You can negotiate "credit-less" stays at individual Marriott hotels. You'll need to pay a room deposit, either for the first night's stay or your entire stay. How much you'll need to deposit will depend on when and where you'll be traveling. You'll need to pay with a money order or a company check, however — Marriott doesn't accept personal checks. Make your Marriott reservation 30 days before you're scheduled to arrive and make sure your deposit is made within seven days after you make your reservation. Otherwise the hotel may reassign your room. Some Marriotts will make late arrival reservations without a deposit. When you travel on business, you can completely bypass the need for a deposit by guaranteeing your room with a corporate credit card and then paying cash for your room on arrival.

Motel 6 (800/466-8356)

Motel 6 offers the best options for prepaying. You can prepay with cash at the Motel 6 closest to you — no matter what Motel 6 location you will be staying at. Or you can send a personal check to the motel location you'll actually be visiting. Just make sure your check arrives at least 14 days before you do. When you check in, you must pay any balance with cash or a money order.

Other Hotel and Motel Chains

Call the major chain you frequent most and ask about their "credit-less" policy — chances are you'll discover that you can easily travel without a credit card. Now, let's see how you can get a rental car without a credit card.

How To Rent A Car Without A Credit Card

A few rental car companies will let you use a debit card (Budget and some Value locations), but most won't accept debit cards. Almost every rental car company, however, has a policy that will let you rent a car without a credit card. One rental car company is much more consumer-friendly than the rest and that's Alamo.

Alamo (800/327-9633)

Alamo is my number one choice for car rentals. Alamo was a very young company when I declared bankruptcy and at that time they were building their business by catering to "credit-less" travelers and "under-25" travelers who have had a hard time renting cars.

Hands down Alamo was — and still is — the BEST rental company for "credit-less" travel. When you travel without credit at Alamo, you don't have to fill out any application form and you don't have to make arrangements months ahead of time.

To pay cash with Alamo, you need to have an airline ticket with the same destination as an Alamo office location and you must make your arrangements at least 24 hours ahead of time. When you pick up your car, you'll need to have a copy of your recent phone bill and a copy of your most recent paycheck stub (or your tax identification number if you're self-employed). You'll pay a deposit of $50 per day (or $200 for a week), in addition to your estimated rental fee. That's all there is to it!

The Other Rental Car Companies

Most rental companies also require that you be at least 25 years old; have a telephone number listed in your name (or a spouse's name) or be able to provide a recent phone bill proving that your number is unlisted; and have been employed at your current job for at least one year. The big kicker is that you must have a clean credit report, showing that your bankruptcy has been discharged and your current accounts are up to-date.

In the past, many people have used debit cards, which take money directly out of their checking accounts, to reserve and pay for rental cars. But most rental car companies won't take debit cars any more. Luckily, there is a way to still get that rental car, even without a debit or credit card.

To rent a car using cash, you'll need to fill out an application. The rental company will check your credit, financial, personal and employment references — so you'll need to have these names, addresses and daytime phone numbers and a copy of your most recent phone bill and paystub with you so the rental car company can easily verify your employment and phone number.

Expect to pay a processing fee of up to $50, plus your estimated rental cost, plus an extra deposit of $100-$500. The deposit is a safety net that covers your unexpected extras: over-the-limit mileage, gasoline or additional days you keep your car. You'll receive the unused portion of your deposit back either the day you turn in your car or within three weeks, depending on the company.

Unfortunately, no rental company accepts cash prepayments at all its locations. Occasionally, you'll even run into credit-happy locations, like Avis in Los Angeles, that will run *another* credit check on you, even if you already cash-qualified with the company.

Start making your "credit-less" car rental plans early on — 90 days before you want to travel if you can, just to be safe. Sometimes the approval process takes that long, sometimes it only takes a few days, but it's better to be safe than sorry! Call the phone numbers listed below to find out!

Avis (800/331-1212)

If you've never cash-qualified with Avis before, start planning 90 days before your trip. The $15 application process takes four to six weeks, but you should allow Avis an extra three weeks to mail you your application. Once you get your "Cash Prepayment Identification Card," you're good to go.

When you're ready to rent from Avis, you'll deposit $300 when you pick up your rental car. If your rental is going to cost more than $300, you'll pay an additional 40% of the total cost. Your rental fee will come out of this deposit. Or, if you end up owing more, you'll pay the balance when you return.

If you'll be traveling for business, your company can set up a corporate account with Avis. This way the rental bill goes directly to your employer and you bypass their prepayment process. Check with your company's payroll officer to see if your employer already has a corporate account.

In addition, Avis offers a great perk if you like to use a travel agent. You can completely bypass their application process if you set up a travel package through your travel agent. This way you pay for the rental car, hotel and airfare in advance by simply writing a check to your travel agent. Your travel agent will then give you vouchers for your rental car and hotel. When you arrive at the counter, you give them the voucher and away you go.

Budget Rent A Car (800/527-0700)

You may be one of the lucky few travelers who are going somewhere Budget accepts cash. Call to check it with a customer service representative before you travel.

Dollar Rent-A-Car (800/327-7607)

Some Dollar locations accept cash, some don't. Their regulations, however, vary from city to city. Call to see if you'll be traveling to a location that accepts cash.

Hertz (800/654-3131)

If you prefer to rent from a big agency, I'd recommend Hertz. You can rent a Hertz car through your travel agent without jumping through all the application hoops. You pay the estimated rental charges, plus a $100-$250 deposit. Your travel agent then pays Hertz with a Miscellaneous Charge Order (MCO), which acts like a check. If your travel agent isn't familiar with an MCO, ask them to call Hertz at 800/331-2456, ext. 7.

If you don't use a travel agent, you'll need to get a "Cash Deposit Identification Card" which shows you're preapproved to pay cash. You'll pay a $15 one-time, non-refundable application fee. Once you're approved, you get your card, which you can use at any Hertz location to pay cash for any size car at any time.

When you rent your car, you must pay a cash advance equal to the estimated rental charges, plus an additional 50% deposit of that estimate (or at least $100). When you return your car, you'll get your 50% deposit back, minus taxes and any additional charges for extra days, mileage or gasoline. Any balance due can be paid with cash, a money order, a personal check or a corporate check.

National Car Rental (800/227-7368)

You can pick up a cash qualification form at any National office, or you can request one over the telephone. After completing the form, mail it to the rental office at your destination. They must receive the form at least two days before you need your car.

You'll pay a non-refundable $50 processing fee, which will count toward your deposit if you're accepted. Having a department store credit card or gasoline credit card will help you, so apply for your gas card using the techniques in Chapter 4. With National, you'll have to pay a minimum deposit of $250, or 150% of your rental cost (for example, a $500 rental would require a $750 deposit). You'll receive a refund for the unused portion of your deposit 7-10 days after you return your car.

Thrifty (800/367-2277)

Some Thrifty locations accept cash prepayment. Call and ask if the Thrifty at your destination accepts cash. If it does, you can then call the location directly to apply.

Two Final Rental Car Tips

If you are traveling on business, you have two additional options open to you:

1. If you already know where you need to spend your days, look through a AAA travel book and see if there is a hotel close to your appointment. This way you can completely avoid renting a car.

2. Have your corporation reserve the rental car for you, and then give you a cash advance to pay the bill. This way you don't have to "cash qualify," you don't have to come up with an additional cash deposit and — best of all — you don't have to front the money for the car rental out of your pocket.

How To Buy Plane Tickets Without A Credit Card

Thanks to modern technology, USAirways (800/428-4322) now accepts payment over the phone using an electronic check transfer. I look for many of the other airlines to follow suit soon, so ask about electronic check transfers when you call and get information about upcoming flights.

Have your checkbook handy when you make your reservation. The airline will ask you for the numbers across the bottom of the check and the name of the bank the check is drawn on. Void that check, tear it up, and record the cost of your airfare in your check register. The airline will then send you a confirmation notice in the mail showing that they took the money out of your checking account. You'll get your tickets in the mail, or you can use "electronic ticketing" and pick them up the day you fly.

Another quick and easy way to pay by cash is to reserve your tickets through a local travel agent. There's no cost to you and you can stop by the agent's office and pay with cash or a check in most cases. Or you can make your reservations directly with the airline and have the travel agent write up the ticket for you. You usually must have the ticket written and paid for within 24 hours of making the reservation.

So, what are you waiting for? Grab your suitcase and start packing. Now you can travel anywhere you want, without worrying about needing a credit card. *Bon Voyage*!

Chapter 8: Action Items

1. Decide what hotel you want to stay at and follow their instructions for credit-less travel.

2. Decide what rental car company you want to use and follow their instructions for credit-less travel.

3. Decide which airline you want to fly and see if they offer electronic check transfers, or book your plane tickets through a travel agent.

chapter 9

When You're Ready To Buy A House

Your next big financial move should be to buy a house if you don't already have one. Once your credit reports are updated, and you've got a secured card that's being reported to your credit bureaus (double check to make sure!), then you can expect to be eligible for a decent interest rate on a home mortgage, within two years of your bankruptcy discharge date.

In general, if you're repaying your debts through a Chapter 13 bankruptcy, your trustee won't let you buy a home until you've finished your repayment plan. But there are exceptions. If you currently have a home, your trustee may allow you to sell your current home, pay some of the equity toward your debts and use the remaining equity as the down payment on a new home, which may or may not be included in your repayment plan.

Once you're ready to buy a home, it's best to start by determining how much house you can afford. Including principal, interest, taxes and insurance, it's a pretty safe estimate that you can afford to pay a mortgage equal to 20% of your pretax income. When you talk to lenders about pre-approval, be up-front about your bankruptcy — and be equally as up-front about the great job you've done rebuilding your credit in a short time.

How Much House Can You Afford?

Lenders will preapprove you for up to 28% of your pretax income, but you may feel like you're stretching to make those payments. For example, with $50,000 in annual pretax income, your lender will likely approve you for a monthly mortgage payment of $1,150. That's 28% of your monthly income, and it would allow you to qualify for a $150,000 loan. At 20%, however, your mortgage payment would be a more manageable $833 – – which would buy you a $120,000 home.

Once you know how much house your lender thinks you can afford, shop for houses that sell for about $20,000 less than his estimate. This will give you a cushion against getting over-extended. My lender told me I could qualify for up to $150,000. So I started shopping for houses in the $125,000 range.

Bottom line, you'll want to pay the lowest payments you can — and as little money up front as you can. That's why I strongly recommend getting an FHA or VA loan. With these loans you make a lower down payment — 3% of the home's selling price, or less. The FHA has also been pretty forgiving in granting mortgages to folks with two-year old bankruptcies. The only drawback is that you generally can only get an FHA loan if the home's value is less than $219,849, unless you're buying in Alaska, Guam, Hawaii or the Virgin Islands, where the cap is $329,774 for a single family home.

If you have had negative credit information added to your credit reports after your bankruptcy, don't despair. You can still become a home-owner, but you'll have to be more creative about how you get your financing. If you can pay a down payment of at least 30% of the home's value, you would improve your chances of getting accepted for a mortgage.

When you find a house you like and you're ready to buy, ask the seller for the name of the company that holds the current mortgage on the house. Then tell the mortgage company:

*"I'm planning on buying the house at
_____ that is owned by _____. I
understand that your company currently holds the
mortgage on this house and I wanted to give you the
opportunity to keep the mortgage. What's the best
rate you offer on a 30-year fixed-rate FHA loan?"*

Be sure to ask how many points are included in that rate
package. Every point tacks an extra 1/8 of a percent onto your
loan's interest rate. When you make an offer to the seller, you can
often split the cost of the points, as well as other costly items like
transfer taxes (more about this in a minute).

Ask your banker and the seller's mortgage holder for an
estimate of closing costs so you can see how much money you'll
need at the closing. Then get a good attorney to help you draw up
a contract that keeps your closing costs low.

Most real estate agents will encourage you to fill out their
contract on the spot and offer it to the seller. Don't do it. The
only way to protect your interests and make sure that you get the
best deal possible is if you have your attorney draw up the contract
— or have a buyer's broker help you draw up a contract and then
have your lawyer review it before you sign anything.

Strategies That Will Help You
Reduce Your Closing Costs

Closing costs can be very expensive — usually from 3%-
6% of the amount you're borrowing. Here are five possible ways
you can reduce your closing costs. I used all five of these techniques and actually wound up getting a check for $1,018 from the
closing attorney. (The first time he'd ever had *that* happen!)

1. *Roll as many of your closing costs into your mortgage as you can.* Some items must be paid separately at the closing, but others can be rolled into your mortgage. Ask your mortgage officer for a list of charges that can be included in your mortgage.

2. *Split closing costs with the seller whenever possible.* Sellers will commonly pay half the points and transfer taxes. But only if you ask.

3. *Roll closing costs into the price of the home.* Ask the seller to let you bump up the price of the house in the contract so you can use the extra money to pay part of your closing costs. Make sure your contract says "Seller agrees to pay an additional $X,XXX to buyer, to be used for closing costs."

4. *Close at the very end of the month.* One expense you will have to pay out-of-your-pocket is your property taxes. These are calculated daily. The closer you are to the end of a month, the fewer days you need to pay for. That's why it makes sense to close on your new home during the last week of the month.

5. *Have the seller pay you at closing for any needed repairs.* The house I bought needed a lot of work. When I had the house inspected, I made a list of 10 repairs that needed to be made. Then I gave the seller two options. Either make the repairs or pay me the cost of the repairs at the time of closing. The seller made some of the repairs and paid me for the others. The total cost of the repairs that still needed to be made was about $4,000. My closing costs were around $3,000. Which means I had $1,000 due me. That's where my $1,018 check came from.

The U.S. Department of Housing and Urban Development (HUD) has a great, FREE booklet called *"Settlement Costs — A HUD Guide, Revised Edition"* that I highly recommend.

You can get your own free copy by calling or writing the U.S. Department of HUD, Attn: RESPA, Room 9146, 451 7th Street SW, Washington, DC 20410-8000; 202/708-4560.

Where To Get Your Down Payment

Most lenders let you borrow 80%-90% of a home's value. This means you'll have to come up with a down payment of 10%-20% of the house's price, in addition to your closing costs. Or you could get an FHA mortgage, where your down payment will be between 3%-5% of your loan amount. With an FHA loan, you can even roll most closing costs into your loan — so the down payment may be your only expense.

The only money I paid out was $3,000, which I used as my down payment for a home with an FHA mortgage. I had saved this money in my company's 401(k) plan. By law, you can withdraw money from a 401(k) account for the down payment on your primary residence — the house you're going to live in.

Withdraw the money instead of borrowing it, for two reasons. First, if you borrow the money you can only tap 50% of your account's value, versus 80% for withdrawing. Second, any money you borrow has to be paid back — and if you stop working for that employer, you'll need to pay all the money back right away. In this day and age, when people are getting laid off left and right, having to live on your savings *and* pay back a retirement plan loan is an extra stress you don't need!

Don't Have Money For A Down Payment?

Another way to get the home of your dreams is to offer the seller the chance to lease the home to you with an option to buy. This will delay your purchase several years — which would give you enough time to qualify for more conventional financing. This way, you'll build up a credit toward whatever purchase price you agree on — rather than just a pile of rent receipts.

Each state has different rules for leasing with an option to buy. Contact your State Consumer Protection Agency to find out the specifics in your area. The paperwork is critical when you choose a lease-option strategy. You'll need a sales document and a lease document and everything must be up to your state's code — which is constantly changing.

Make sure that the sales document states that you can buy the house at the home's appraised value as of the time you exercise your option, or at the sales price as of the date the lease option is dated, whichever is less. This way, you won't pay more than the home's fair market value if you exercise your option.

Generally, with a lease-option, you rent a home for two to three years and a portion of your rent gets set aside until you build up enough savings to pay the down payment. In addition, those two years give you enough time to qualify for more conventional financing. Of course, if you decide to move before you exercise your option and before you actually buy the home, you'll forfeit any money that's been set aside.

Other Strategies For Buying a Home After Bankruptcy

There are a few other strategies you can use to get the house of your dreams after your bankruptcy, if you don't have the money for a down payment. Both of these strategies work very well if the seller of the home you want to buy isn't strapped for cash and would welcome a steady stream of income from you, while you restore your credit enough to qualify for a mortgage.

1. *Seller Take-Back Mortgage.* Take-back mortgages are usually second mortgages, but it's becoming more commonplace to see private sellers offering first mortgages as take-backs. Usually this happens when the sellers have paid off their mortgage and also already own the home that they are moving to.

You have two options with a take-back mortgage. The seller may be willing to offer you an "interest-only" mortgage at the going interest rate, where you only pay interest — you don't pay any principal for several years. Instead, the loan is a balloon loan, where you would owe the total loan amount at the end of a set period, say five years. This would give you enough time to get qualified for a conventional loan. The second option is more like a regular mortgage, where you pay principal and interest. Either way, the seller earns a steady stream of income from the home. If you default on the loan, the seller can foreclose on the property.

Many sellers used to shy away from take-back mortgages, because they would have to keep track of your mortgage payments, initiate collections and foreclosure procedures if you defaulted, and all that other tedious stuff. Now, however, if the seller has a mortgage lender draw up the papers, uses the standardized forms and meets a few other requirements, the seller can then sell the loan to Fannie Mae, instead of having to collect monthly payments from you. This means that sellers can offer take-back mortgages without having to tie up all their equity for several years.

2. *Land Contracts.* This deferred sales agreement between you and the seller of the home is only available in some states. With a land contract, you both agree on a time by which you must come up with your own financing to take the property off the

seller's hands. You move into the home and make monthly payments to the seller. Although the seller isn't legally the owner, he or she is still considered the owner of the home by the mortgage company in most states. So the loan is still technically still the seller's debt and will be reported on the seller's credit report.

Generally, you'll have to come up with some cash to buy out the seller's equity (either all or part of it, depending on how quickly the seller wants to get cash out of his property). If you can't finance the house by the agreed upon date, the land contract expires and the property continues to be the responsibility of the seller, although the seller may legally have to sue you to get clear title to the property. If you decide to use a land contract, hire an attorney to draw up the contract to make sure that everything is done correctly. Not all mortgage holders will agree to a land contract, but the industry is changing rapidly. VA loans, in particular, are good choices for land contracts.

> *Jerry, a computer expert with the military in Virginia Beach, used a land contract to buy his dream house recently. He closed on his house with a land contract shortly after bankruptcy. Eighteen months later he was able to get a mortgage on his own at an affordable interest rate. You can too!*

Start by looking for "For-Sale-By-Owner" homes that have been on the market for a few months and ask the seller if they would consider a Land Contract arrangement.

Refinancing After Bankruptcy

I didn't own a home when I declared bankruptcy, but many people do. If you're a homeowner, and you want to refinance after your bankruptcy has been discharged, you can. And you can avoid paying an out-of-this-world interest rate if you follow the strategies you've read about so far — rebuilding your credit before you apply to refinance.

Basically, the longer it's been since your bankruptcy, the better. If you try to refinance within a year of your bankruptcy you're likely to pay through the nose. Work to rebuild your credit over a year or two, though, and you'll get a much more reasonable interest rate. Lenders I talked to were very up-front about what you can expect when you apply for a mortgage after bankruptcy.

Bottom line: If you discharged your debts under Chapter 7, you'll be considered an A+ borrower 24 months after your bankruptcy is discharged. This assumes that you have no new *negative* credit information on your credit reports, and you have to have some new *positive* credit information on your credit reports.

Time isn't the only factor that mortgage refinancing companies look at, however. You also need to show that you've re-established your credit — with a secured credit card that doesn't report as secured, a gas card and a car loan. You can safely rebuild your credit so it puts you in the best possible light, and shows the refinancing company that you're a good credit risk. Use your credit card for small purchases every month, and pay the bill off in full each month.

Don't run up big bills on your credit cards or start carrying a balance from month to month or the mortgage lender will assume that you've gotten yourself back into the same debt cycle you were in before you declared bankruptcy. Instead, show them with your payment history that you've turned over a new leaf.

What Type of Mortgage Lender Should You Use?

There are basically two types of mortgage lenders — "A-list" lenders and "BCD-lenders." The worse your credit report looks, the further down the alphabet you go. That's why it's so important that you rebuild your credit until you're back on the "A" or "B" list before you refinance.

When you're ready to refinance, call several different mortgage loan brokers and tell them you're looking for competitive refinancing rates. Don't go to anyone who specializes in "bad credit" mortgage refinancing. You want a mortgage broker who deals with "A" lenders who have access to BCD sources. Any good mortgage broker gets paid out of the loan proceeds, so don't let any mortgage broker talk you into paying them anything simply to meet with you.

The mortgage broker will probably have you fill out a mini loan application to see where you fit, creditwise. Be up-front about your past bankruptcy. A good mortgage broker will help you put your best foot forward for the lender, even going so far as to help you write a letter of explanation about the circumstances surrounding your bankruptcy.

Some mortgage brokers, however, will try to label you as a "subprime borrower" in order to charge you a higher interest rate. You'll be able to spot these lenders right away. They'll sound something like this: *"Oh, well, I see you have a bankruptcy here. Hmmm... That will make it more difficult to get you approved for a loan. We can still get you a mortgage, but you're gonna have to pay a higher interest rate, of course... because of this bankruptcy here."*

These lenders will talk in circles, trying to use your guilt to justify charging you more interest. Don't fall for this ploy. After your bankruptcy has been discharged for two years, and assuming you don't have any new late payments on your credit report, you can qualify for the same interest rate as everyone else.

If overpaying interest on your loan doesn't scare you away from these lenders, here's another way some mortgage lenders will try and charge you more money, simply because they're counting on you feeling guilty over declaring bankruptcy. Many subprime loans also include a pre-payment penalty. After a few years of paying a higher interest, when you go to refinance at a more reasonable interest rate, you could get a nasty surprise when you discover that you now have to pay a penalty which could range from 3% of the outstanding loan ($3,000 on a $100,000 loan balance) to six months' of interest (about $4,800 on a $100,000 loan at 8.5%).

If you've had good credit since your bankruptcy, with at least a year or two's worth of on-time payments, or if you reaffirmed a car loan and have had at least six month's worth of on-time payments, you should be able to get a decent interest rate. If you run into a mortgage lender who wants to steer you to a higher interest rate. Politely but firmly say: *"I know I have enough credit references to qualify for the going market rate. Since you're not able to approve a loan at that rate, I don't want to waste any more of your time."* Then pick up your papers and walk out the door. Remember: no creditor can humiliate you unless you let yourself be humiliated. Even after bankruptcy, you can get a good deal from the lenders that are used by the better mortgage brokerages.

Mortgage brokerages that have solid reputations in the industry include SunTrust, Prestige Mortgage Services and Universal American Mortgage Company (UAMC). Look in your yellow pages under "mortgage brokers" for a local branch of these or other large, reputable mortgage brokers. They can use a wide variety of lenders — and their experienced mortgage brokers can walk you through the process and help you get a competitive mortgage.

Mortgage brokers deal with lenders who offer new mortgages, refinances and equity loans, all from ABCD sources. The type of loan you'll qualify for will depend on how well you follow the steps in this book and rebuild your credit.

For example, if you're looking to get a first-time mortgage, your bankruptcy needs to be discharged for at least 12 months if you want a decent interest rate; 24 months would qualify you for the going interest rate that everyone else is paying, if you've used the steps in this book to rebuild your credit.

You'll need to have some new credit history in front of your bankruptcy, with a VISA or MasterCard that you've made on-time payments with for at least 12 months. Any other type of on-time credit history after the bankruptcy, such as keeping student loans current, or paying on a reaffirmed car loan on time over 6-12 months, will also help you qualify for a first-time mortgage as early as one year after your bankruptcy is discharged. With this type of good credit history in front of your bankruptcy, you should be able to qualify for an A-loan. I recommend calling the various mortgage brokers for a free financial analysis. They can look at your entire financial situation and determine whether or not they can help you. Then they'll tell you all your options.

If you're looking to get a mortgage and you had a foreclosure before you declared bankruptcy, you can still qualify for credit from an A- or B-lender, as long as you've taken the other steps toward rebuilding your credit, as listed above.

When you're looking to refinance after declaring bankruptcy, it pays to have kept your mortgage as current as possible. Mortgage lenders look most closely at your last 12 months' history on your mortgages. The fewer 30-day late pays you've had in the past year, the lower interest you'll get when you refinance. You'll generally qualify for a refinance loan from a C-lender if your mortgage payments haven't been 30 days late more than four times, or more than 60 days late one time in the last 12 months. If you've got fewer late pays than that showing on your current mortgage, and you can't wait a full year to refinance, there's still hope!

Don't worry if you can't wait a full year to get some of the extra late pays to be more than a year old. With many mortgage brokers, you can get a loan from one lending source and after two years of good payments, you can have the interest rate lowered.

How to Buy a Home Less Than a Year After Bankruptcy

You may find that it's necessary for you to relocate after your bankruptcy and you may want to buy a home sooner than the one to two years you would have to wait to restore your credit after bankruptcy. Luckily, you still have several options:

1. *Take over an existing loan on a property that's worth less than the current mortgage.* Especially in areas where property values fell sharply — like Southern California — you can find homeowners who are "upside-down" on their mortgage. They owe more than the home is worth, and especially if prices are starting to rise again, this might be a good time to buy such a home. Sometimes, you won't even need to come up with a down payment in order to take over a loan like this. Instead, you may only need to

come up with enough to bring the defaulted loan current, which could be just a few thousand dollars.

2. *Get a non-conforming mortgage.* Many lenders offer "non-conforming" loans, which let you qualify for a mortgage soon after your bankruptcy is discharged. You may be required to pay a down payment of 25% or more, and your interest rate will be in the double digits. If you decide to go with a non-conforming mortgage, make sure that the interest rate is automatically reduced after several years of good payments on your part, or make sure that you're guaranteed the opportunity to refinance at a lower interest rate after two years of good payments. Non-conforming mortgages are issued by "CD" lenders. If you go this route, expect to pay an interest rate of around 13% and have to come up with a down payment of at least 20%.

Chapter 9: Action Items

1. Figure out how much house you can afford to buy.

2. Decide how much down payment you'll need — and where you can get your down payment from.

3. Decide if you'll need to use a "no-down payment" option, like lease-to-own.

4. Shop for the best mortgage lender.

5. Make sure you know exactly what your credit reports say about you.

chapter 10

What If You Find Yourself In Over Your Head Again?

If you find yourself in debt over your head again, don't panic. I know it's hard to think about being in debt again, but there is a way out!

If things are just a little tight, there's a quick and easy strategy you can use to start getting things back on track and stop having to live paycheck to paycheck. First, stop charging for 30 days. Put the credit cards in the freezer in a plastic bag filled with water and don't even think about using them. You may find that this is all you need to do to get back on track.

Most of us get stuck in "debt management" rather than "debt repayment." Debt management is where you send in a $200 payment to a credit card, but you charge $210 that month (or more), and when you get your new bill, you still owe the same amount. Sticking your credit cards in the freezer, where you can't add any new debt to them, will help you get out of debt faster.

In addition to not charging on credit cards, it's also important not to borrow money during the 30 days either. This is a common mistake people make when they stop charging. They figure they can pay back people when more money comes in. Avoid "buy now, pay later" offers that come to you. Whether you're buying a magazine subscription or a new dining room set, don't buy it unless you have the money to pay for it now.

I know it can be very scary to try and live only on the cash you make. If you start having difficulty making ends meet, don't panic. And don't automatically assume that you have to sacrifice everything in your life to avoid taking on new debt. The most important debts are your secured debts — your car loan and your mortgage or rent. Once you've paid for those each month, use your remaining income for daily living expenses — food, insurance, gasoline, utilities. Finally, use your remaining income to pay a little something toward each of your unsecured debts so you don't jeopardize your home or your family's well-being.

Short-Term Strategies To Help You Get Back On Track

As you work to build up more income, and pare down your expenses, you might want to incorporate some of these short-term strategies into your life:

1. *Sell Items You Can Do Without.* Start with the big items, then look to sell smaller items. Garage sales, consignment shops, flea markets and free newspaper advertisements are all great places to sell small — and big items.

You'll be surprised at all the books, videos, extra electronic equipment and appliances, clothes and sports equipment that are cluttering up your home. Start small, so you don't get too overwhelmed at once. Take one box, one drawer, one room at a time. You'll be surprised at how much more motivated you'll be once you convert your first batch of clutter into cold hard cash!

If you're not sure it's a good idea to sell a big item, calculate what it costs you to own the item, versus what it would cost to rent it for the same number of days you used it.

For example, say you have a boat. Write down how many days you spent on the boat in the past 12 months. Don't include days you spent cleaning, etc. Only include days you actually had fun on the boat. Then write down how much you've paid out on the boat in the past 12 months. Include any monthly payments, dockage fees, and supplies. Then add in an hourly rate for time spent maintaining the boat. This will tell you how much you've "paid" to own the boat this year.

Next, call around and find out how much it would have cost you to rent a boat for the number of days you used it. Now you can easily see which costs you more right now — renting or owning. If it's less expensive to rent, it makes more financial sense to sell the boat rather than keep it.

I understand that your big ticket item, like a boat or a classic car or a motorcycle, has sentimental value and it makes you feel good — but right now it may be causing a drain on your finances. You're always better off getting the best price you can while you're in control of the situation. If people ask why you're getting rid of these items, just say, *"You know, I just got tired of them. Figured someone else could enjoy having them more than I'm enjoying them now.* Down the road, when you've got your finances back under control, you can replace these items, or buy even better toys — for cash — and not have the debt hanging over your head.

Do you have a car with a loan that's "upside down," where you owe more on the car than it's worth? If so, try selling the car. When you find a buyer for your car, negotiate a price, and make sure the buyer is approved for financing. Then call your lender, tell the lender that you have a buyer, and how much they're willing to pay, and negotiate with your lender to see if you can pay a lower monthly payment on the remaining amount.

Your lender may be very interested in this option, since he/she doesn't want to have to repossess the car or have you fall behind on payments. Remember: If the first person you talk to can't help you, keep asking to be transferred until you get to someone who has the authority to work with you.

2. *Give Yourself and Your Family Members A Temporary Allowance.* This may sound odd, or controlling, but it can be a lifesaver. Most of us spend an enormous amount of money each day or each week on "stuff." You know the feeling. You leave home with $20 and by the end of the day you're broke — and you've got nothing to show for the $20 you spent, right?

Make sure that both you and your spouse are okay with setting up an allowance situation, so one of you doesn't come across as a "disciplining parent" and the other one as a "punished child." Money can carry a lot of emotional weight, so talk through what's being triggered when you bring up the subject of cutting back on money.

Cutting back on things you "want" can push some buttons. So try to keep in mind this important thought: Cutting back or eliminating the things you "want" now, for the next six months, will make it possible for you to have many more of the things you "want" for the rest of your life. If you don't take action now, you'll always have to pick and choose between the things you "want." Set up a temporary allowance and the end result will be permanent prosperity.

3. *Boost Your Income Renting Out Space.* Another suggestion that might offer immediate relief is to rent out a room in your house. I know that giving up privacy is a hard thing to do, but it will provide you with some much needed cash that can break the debt cycle. Two good places to find short-term rentals

are local universities or hospitals. Call the public affairs offices at the university or hospitals near you to see if there is a need for short-term rentals in your area. You might also be able to make a little extra money by renting out garage space to someone who needs a place to store a vehicle, or a place to work on a large project.

4. *Track Your Expenses For One Month.* Get a shoebox and put it on the kitchen table and tell everyone in your family to put receipts for EVERYTHING into the shoebox. If you use a vending machine at work, immediately take a scrap of paper, write down "Soda, 50-cents" and the date, then stick it in your wallet or your pocket. When you get home, empty your pockets right into the shoebox.

At the end of the month, sit down and write out what your expenses and income were that month, so you can figure out where you're spending your money. This lets you see where you're spending more money than you want to on stuff you don't want. You can then free up some of that money to pay down debts, or pay for the things you DO want!

For a really good do-it-yourself program, I recommend getting a copy of *The Budget Kit: The Common Cent$ Money Management Workbook* by Judy Lawrence (ISS Publications, $16.95 + s/h, 800/688-1960; 1925 Juan Tabo NE, Suite B249, Albuquerque, NM 87112). This 8-1/2 x 11 workbook is straight-forward, easy to use and will help you prepare for both expected and unexpected expenses throughout the year.

Judy is also the author of *The Money Tracker.* (ISS Publications, $15.95 + s/h, 800/688-1960; 1925 Juan Tabo NE, Suite B249, Albuquerque, NM 87112). You can carry this pocket-sized hardback with you to track your expenses, instead of using the shoe-box method. *The Money Tracker* includes a monthly section to help you identify your "money triggers" and explore your emotions when you spend money. The book also has a "splurge diary" and money journal.

5. *Examine where you're spending more money than you need to on necessities.* There are some necessities, such as insurance, that you shouldn't scrimp on. But that's not to say that you have to overpay for them, either. For instance, premiums on term life insurance are much lower than premiums on insurance that builds up a cash value (such as whole life, variable life or universal life insurance).

One place to cut monthly costs is to buy a term life insurance policy to replace your cash value life insurance policy. There are several good insurance companies that sell term life insurance without charging a commission. You simply apply for the insurance and, once you're accepted, cash out of your old policy.

To cancel your old policy, write your old insurance company and ask them to send you cancellation forms and forms for the return of any cash value. Send your letter certified, return receipt requested. You should hear back within 2-3 weeks. If not, call your insurance agent.

Once you receive the cash value that's owed to you, you then can use part of the money to pay your premiums (or prepay your premium for the entire next year) and then use the rest to pay your daily living expenses, or to pay off your debt.

You can get a quote from a variety of high-quality, low-fee insurance companies by calling Insurance Information, Inc. at

800/472-5800 or 508/394-9117. Your best bet will be to get a policy with a 10-year renewable term, guaranteed to age 70.

6. *Use the DebtBuster Strategy* if you can "do-it-yourself," or see a credit counselor. The DebtBuster Strategy, on page 67, will help you see at a glance who you owe and how much you owe. It will also help you work out a realistic way to pay off those debts, in as little as one year. If this is too difficult, then I encourage you to go see a credit or budget counselor.

You're not alone if you can't set up or stick to a budget. Budget counselor Judy Lawrence (who wrote *The Budget Kit* and *The Money Tracker*) works with a variety of clients and specializes in budget counseling for the wealthy. She had an heiress who receives over a million dollars a year from her trust fund — and couldn't make ends meet. Judy got her to work within a budget of $20,000 a month, and now she's able to save money, donate money to charitable causes and still do the things she wants to do.

It just goes to show you that no matter how much money you have, it won't ever be enough if you don't have a solid plan outlining where you want to spend your money. Most of us haven't learned how to make a budget work for us — instead we're constantly trying to cram our expenses into an unrealistic budget. If you're uncomfortable seeing a credit counselor, you might want to use a private budget counselor who comes to your home and works with you to set up a budget. Check your yellow pages for budget counselors.

Most of what credit and budget counselors do you can do for yourself. But if you're too emotionally involved with your money situation to create and stick with a plan and negotiate with your creditors, then going through a credit counselor may be a good option for you. Sometimes it just helps to have a third party acting as a go-between. You can even give creditors permission to talk to a spouse or a friend who isn't emotionally involved, if talking to your creditors upsets you too much.

Credit counselors, including those who are listed as Consumer Credit Counseling Services (CCCS) or National Credit Counseling Services (NCCS, now Genus), are nonprofit organizations that offer free budget counseling and, for a small fee, debt repayment programs. These companies will also negotiate with your creditors, who may report this fact on your credit reports.

Call the credit counselor to make an appointment and bring all your paperwork with you, showing your expenses and your income. At your appointment, you'll meet with a counselor who will conduct an in-depth interview with you, to help you set up a household budget separating your needs from your wants.

That budget counseling session may be all you'll need. Or you may want to continue working with a counselor to set up a debt repayment program. There are many good independent counseling services, as well as those that are listed as a Consumer Credit Counseling Service (CCCS). I'll give you a complete rundown of the top credit and budget counselors I've come across later in this chapter.

Do You Find It Hard To
Stop Spending More Than You Make?

Declaring bankruptcy and getting out of debt are incredibly empowering things to do. But they won't do you any good at all if you still find yourself spending more than you make. You'll find yourself caught in the same vicious circle eventually. If this happens to you, I urge you to pick up a copy of *How to Get Out of Debt, Stay Out of Debt and Live Prosperously*, by Jerrold Mundis.

If habitual overspending stops you from digging your way out of debt, you may be a compulsive spender and Debtors Anonymous can help. Debtors Anonymous is a 12-step program that can offer you support and guidance in overcoming a barrier to your financial recovery. You do not need to actually be in debt to be a member of DA. The only requirement for membership in DA is a willingness to stop incurring unsecured debt.

There are many reasons people are drawn to Debtors Anonymous. Business failures, a pattern of bouncing checks, excessive student loans, unpaid taxes, gambling, real estate losses, even messy divorces are good reasons to attend DA meetings.

Debtors Anonymous groups can often be supportive, but be forewarned that there are factions of DA that frown on bankruptcy. Mostly this attitude comes from all the people they see come through the doors several years after bankruptcy, in debt up to their eyeballs. Don't let that deter you from getting the support you need. You can start a new trend of DA members who join up right after bankruptcy and remain solvent for the rest of your life! Check your local newspapers and community center listings for meetings in your area.

You can also find out about meetings in your area by sending a self-addressed, stamped business-sized envelope to: The General Service Board of Debtors Anonymous, P.O. Box 888, Needham, MA 02492. To find a contact number for a meeting near you, I'd also recommend visiting http://www.solvency.org. Debtors Anonymous also has a wonderful website that you might want to visit: http://www.debtorsanonymous.org.

You're not alone if you spend money to make yourself feel better. But there are other, more constructive ways you can deal with personal problems besides running to the nearest store and buying something, or buying gifts as a way of expressing your love, or buying gifts in order to be "accepted" by others.

Today, you can start to change your habits a little at a time. When you get the urge to buy something to make yourself feel better, slow down, take a deep breath, go for a walk, garden, putter around the house, take a hot bath, or even clean out some clutter in your life — you may just find something you'd forgotten you owned, which is almost as good as going out and buying something new to begin with.

Compulsive gambling could also be an obstacle to your financial security. Compulsive gambling is a serious illness that creates mountains of problems, financial and emotional. You're not alone if you have a gambling problem. The United States Department of Public Health estimates that there are six to ten million Americans, men and women alike, who suffer from compulsive gambling.

Could You Have a Gambling Problem?

If you're wondering if you might have a gambling problem, or like to gamble but don't think it's a problem for you, I encourage you to honestly answer the following twenty questions, just to be on the safe side:

1. Do you ever take time off work to go gambling or to recuperate from gambling?

2. Has gambling made your home life unhappy?

3. Has gambling affected your reputation?

4. Have you ever felt bad after gambling?

5. Do you ever gamble to get money to pay debts or solve financial difficulties?

6. Does gambling cause a decrease in your ambition, or your efficiency?

7. After losing, do you feel you must return as soon as possible so you can win back your losses?

8. After a win, do you have a strong urge to win more?

9. Do you often gamble until your last dollar is gone?

10. Do you ever borrow money to finance your gambling or to pay for something that you couldn't afford to buy yourself, because of your gambling losses?

11. Have you ever sold or pawned anything to gamble?

12. Are you reluctant to use "gambling money" for normal expenditures?

13. Does gambling make you careless about the welfare of yourself or your family?

14. Do you ever gamble longer than you had planned?

15. Have you ever gambled to escape worry or trouble?

16. Have you ever considered committing an illegal act to finance your gambling?

17. Does gambling cause you to have difficulty sleeping?

18. When you have an argument, disappointment or frustration, do you get an urge to gamble to make yourself feel better?

19. Do you ever have an urge to celebrate any good fortune with a few hours of gambling?

20. Have you ever considered suicide as a result of your gambling?

How did you do? Most compulsive gamblers will answer "yes" to at least seven of these questions. If you think you may have a gambling problem, I encourage you to contact Gamblers Anonymous, a 12-step support program that is open, free-of-charge to people who have a desire to stop gambling. Groups meet all over the country. To get information about meetings in your area call 213/386-8789; or write: Gamblers Anonymous International Service Office; P.O. Box 17173; Los Angeles, CA 90017.

How to Keep From Falling Back Into Debt

If you find yourself in a financial crunch down the road — say you get laid off unexpectedly (which happened to me!) — you can still easily keep yourself from getting back into debt. Don't let yourself get overwhelmed by the *total* amount you owe. Instead, break the debt down into manageable chunks. This will help you get yourself back up-to-date on your bills.

For some bills, you can make payments that are smaller than the monthly requirement until you regain your financial footing. Even a $5 or $10 payment shows that you're making a good faith effort. Try to send at least $5 to each of your creditors every month. By making small payments you let the creditor know that you are trying to catch up.

It's important, though, that you don't let late fees and missed payment fees pile up, or you'll be taking one step forward and two steps back. Follow the steps below and you'll keep moving forward.

Call Your Creditors and Get a New Repayment Schedule

If you find yourself falling behind with your creditors, *call your creditors and ask them to negotiate a new repayment schedule with you.* Do this before your creditors start calling you. Sit down, work up a budget with your daily living expenses. Determine how much you can realistically pay each creditor and how long it will take you to resume your regular payment schedule.

Then call your creditors, or ask a friend or relative to call on your behalf (be sure to tell your creditor that your friend is authorized to talk to them, or this won't work). When you call, explain your situation calmly, and propose your modified payment plan. For example, you might offer to pay 50% of your normal payment for three months and then resume your regular payment amount.

Some creditors are starting to realize that working out these "hardship payment plans" is in their best interest. One woman found that Citibank was helpful — and her willingness to stick to her guns about how much she could pay each month created a "win-win" situation for both her and her creditor:

*My [Citibank] account was chronically
delinquent due to a failed business. They placed me
on a hardship program with a 5% interest rate and
a monthly payment of $85. My balance is $5,500.
The hardship program is set up for six months at a
time, and then the payments revert back to the
original amount and interest, once the account is
no longer delinquent.*

*I have gone through the cycle of making six
regular payments and then not making the higher
payments and being placed back on the hardship
program several times. Citibank just reviewed AND
renewed my hardship payment. They will get twelve
payments in a row instead of six. I get 5% interest
and a payment I can afford.*

*Call them and tell them your financial
situation. Ask about the hardship program and
explain how much you can afford. They take what
you can pay or they get nothing. Stand your ground
and they will listen to you.*

Write down the name of the person you talked to, the date
and time, and what you agreed to do. You may or may not be
successful with the first person you talk to. Do not be discouraged! Remember: Your goal is to get the creditor to say "Yes!" to
your repayment plan. Faced with a choice of no money or some
money, your creditor is eventually going to work with you. If you
get turned down, politely ask to speak to the person who has the
authority to work out a deal with you. And *never, ever* agree to
pay more than you *know* you can pay the creditor each month.
Once you break an agreement with a creditor, they are much less
likely to work with you on a repayment plan.

So if you think you can afford to send $50, but that might put you in a pinch, stick to your guns and say *"I know I can pay you $25 a month."* If they ask for $50, simply say, *"I'd like to agree to $50 a month, but that's just not realistic. And I don't want you to be disappointed in me if I can't come up with that amount some month. I can commit to $25 a month and will send extra money whenever I can."* Letting your creditors know up-front that your word is important to you will strengthen your credibility.

Once your creditor agrees on the phone to your reduced payment plan, *write a follow-up letter to the person you spoke with to confirm your agreement.* Be sure to keep a copy of the letter for your records. Send the letter via certified mail, return receipt requested, so you have proof that the letter was received.

Write Your Creditors If That's More Comfortable

If you're uncomfortable asking for help from your creditors over the phone, send them the following letter as soon as you realize you're going to miss a payment (or as soon as you can once you've missed a payment):

(Date)

[Creditor]
[Address]
[City, State, Zip]
Re: [Your account number]

Dear Sir/Madam:

My financial situation has changed unexpectedly because [I was laid off, lost my job, had a medical crisis, was divorced, etc.]. I cannot currently make the minimum payments required on this account and am asking for your assistance in getting this bill paid.

I have a solid payment history with your company [note if you're currently behind], and I want to keep my good credit with you. I see two possible solutions to this problem, and I have listed them in order of which would work best for me.

1. I would like to request a 60 day deferral, allowing me to skip two payments. (If your account is already behind, ask for a 90 day deferral). I trust that you would reage the account so that it remains current and that the skipped payments would not be reported as past due.

OR

2. I would like to request that the interest be frozen and the minimum payment be cut in half for the next six to twelve months. This would give me enough time to make adjustments in my budget so I can begin repaying my account.

I apologize for the inconvenience, but I hope you can help me get through this difficult time. Please send me your written reply and call me within the next 10 days to let me know which option is best for you, so I can budget the payment amount. You can reach me at [your phone number]. The best time to call is [best time to call you].

Thank you again.

Sincerely,

[Your name]

This letter will help you get caught up with most creditors, without damaging your newly reborn credit rating. If you have creditors who won't work with you, and continually hound you with telephone calls, you may need to be more proactive with your creditors. Send them the following certified letter:

(Date)

[Creditor]
[Address]
[City, State, Zip]
Re: [Your account number]

Dear Sir/Madam:

I have attempted to work out a repayment plan with you which would satisfy your need to have my debt to you repaid, without my having to declare bankruptcy or default on this debt entirely.

To date, you have been unwilling to work with me to make this repayment plan a possibility. Instead, you continue to make harassing phone calls demanding repayment of this debt.

I am writing you today to let you know that it is inconvenient for you to phone me at home or work, or to contact anyone associated with me, whether they be neighbors, co-workers or anyone else. As of the date you receive this letter, all further contact with me must be in writing to my billing address. No other contact should be made by you to me or to anyone I know regarding this debt.

As you know, any future calls from you will be a violation of my rights as a consumer, and I will exercise my rights to their fullest extent, including bringing suit against you for violation of the Fair Debt Collection Act.

As I have told you in the past, my financial situation has changed unexpectedly because [I was laid off, lost my job, had a medical crisis, was divorced, etc.]. I cannot currently make the minimum payments required on this account and am asking for your assistance in getting this bill paid using the repayment plan I have worked out.

I trust that you will work with me, in writing, to develop a repayment plan that will allow this debt to be repaid over time.

Thank you again.

Sincerely,

[Your name]

Be sure to send this letter certified, return receipt requested. Include a copy of your original letter to the creditor, with your suggested repayment plan. Once the creditor has signed for the letter, you are then in a position to sue them if they attempt to contact you or anyone else by phone, to talk about your debt. Every time a creditor violates your rights by attempting to contact you over the phone, you can sue them for a minimum of $1,000. Once a creditor realizes that you know your rights and won't be harassed, they'll be much more likely to work out a repayment plan with you that you can afford.

What If You Fall Behind On Your Mortgage?

Less than one year after I bought my home and started renovations, I was laid off from my job. Between unemployment and my savings, I was able to pay my mortgage for six months. The month I first knew that I would not be able to make my mortgage payment, I called my mortgage lender who suggested that I call HUD because my loan was an FHA loan. On FHA loans, HUD is the private mortgage insurer, which means that HUD insures FHA loans against nonpayment.

The first thing the HUD representative said to me was, *I wish you'd called us right after you got laid off instead of using up your savings to pay your mortgage!* It turned out that because I had an FHA loan, I was eligible for "HUD Assignment," which meant that HUD bought my mortgage from my lender and gave me three years to get back on my feet.

Depending on your financial situation, your monthly payments under HUD assignment could range from zero to a small portion of your current mortgage, for up to three years. At the end of the three years, the missed mortgage payments are tacked onto the back end of your mortgage. So, basically you turn your 30-year mortgage into a 33-year mortgage.

HUD has scaled back considerably with its assignment program, and has resold many of its loans to other mortgage lenders. But you may still qualify, so I wanted to let you know what to expect. If you have an FHA loan, call your lender and ask to be connected to the Loan Counseling or Loss Mitigation department. When you reach a loan counselor, say *"I want to apply for HUD assignment."*

Your loan counselor will then hook you up with a HUD counselor. If your loan is approved for assignment to HUD, HUD will become your new lender. The current terms and remaining loan amount will stay the same, as will your interest rate. However, you could be eligible for three years of reduced or suspended payments. Once you've missed three of your regular mortgage payments, HUD will start reviewing your case for assignment. While your case is being reviewed, your lender cannot take steps to foreclose on your home.

While you're being considered for HUD assignment, your lender will call each month, just to verify that you're living in the home; if you vacate the home, you lose your right to be considered for HUD assignment. Having you in your home is added protection for your lender, so don't dread these calls. They're just checking in with you.

One of the first things my HUD counselor told me was to not be alarmed if I got turned down for HUD assignment. She said that a high percentage of cases are initially turned down, at least once or twice. If you get turned down when you've applied for HUD assignment, follow the appeals process listed on the back of the papers you receive. I was fortunate — my application for HUD assignment joined a growing stack of applications during the government furlough. When the government finally got back to business, they must have realized that all those appeals created more work for them. As a result, my application was approved on the first try. So don't give up if you get turned down. Work with your HUD counselor — he or she will be glad to walk you through the steps you need to take.

Once you get approved for HUD assignment, you'll be asked to fill out a financial statement detailing your income, expenses, and various debts. List everyone you owe money to, so HUD gets a total picture of what your income and expenses look like. You'll also have to provide a copy of your last tax return and your estimated income for the coming year. HUD will then use this information to calculate what your payments will be for the coming year. You will then get a formal payment plan agreement from HUD. Sign both copies and return one copy, via certified mail, to HUD. Follow the terms of the payment plan exactly and make your payments on time every month.

You can then use the time you're in the repayment plan to catch up on your other bills, pay off other debts and get back on your feet. Once the three year forbearance period is up, you'll have to start making your regular mortgage payment again, or risk losing your home. So use this time to your advantage. The strategies outlined in this chapter will help you take the steps necessary to get back on track before your assignment ends.

As I mentioned earlier, HUD can resell your assigned loan to a private mortgage lender. By law, the new lender must honor the terms of the forbearance agreements set up under HUD. Some of these lenders, however, will try to bully you into believing that they can foreclose on the loan, or demand full repayment of the money you tacked onto the end of the loan. If your HUD assignment is sold, and the new lender threatens you with foreclosure or demands repayment in full for the mortgage payments you didn't make during the forbearance agreement, immediately contact your HUD counselor and ask what steps you should take. If the new lender is in violation of the original forbearance agreement, and you made all the payments required by you under the forbearance agreement, you may have the right to sue the new lender to protect your home from foreclosure.

What If You Don't Have an FHA Mortgage?

If your financial circumstances change and you believe you will soon fall behind on your mortgage, you may still have protection from foreclosure, even if you don't have an FHA mortgage. Most of us, when we buy a home, also buy something called "Private Mortgage Insurance" or PMI. Mortgage lenders require you to buy PMI until you have at least 20% worth of equity built up in your home. Private mortgage insurance protects your lender against default by you. But what most people don't know is that PMI can also protect you against foreclosure.

How exactly does PMI work? Well, if you default on your loan, your PMI will pay your lender a foreclosure claim, to offset the loss the lender may have suffered. Usually, this amount is more than the mortgage payments you've missed. Your PMI insurer may find that it is less expensive for them to advance you enough money to cover your missed payments, if you're in a position to start making payments again.

Also, if you need to sell your home, even if you're "upside-down" on your mortgage and owe more than the home is worth, PMI can come to your rescue. In these cases, the PMI issuer would pay off part of your remaining mortgage, so that you won't still owe the lender money after your home is sold. If you decide to use this strategy, I strongly recommend that you first consult an experienced real estate and/or tax attorney before you get started. Otherwise, you could wind up with "phantom income" that will be reported to the IRS — and on which you'll have to pay taxes.

How to Contact and Work With Your PMI Insurer

Your first step, if you need assistance from your PMI company, is to contact the Workout Department at the PMI insurer. Tell the insurer that you believe it will cost them less money to help you than to pay off your mortgage lender's claim after foreclosure. In order to have your PMI insurer help you, your missed mortgage payments must be due to circumstances beyond your control — such as a death or illness, a divorce or loss of a job. If your PMI insurer agrees, they may pay your lender the money needed to bring your mortgage up-to-date. You then repay the PMI insurer. Usually, your repayment is based on your ability to repay — and you generally aren't charged any interest during repayment.

Call your mortgage lender and ask them who your private mortgage insurer is. If your lender is reluctant to reveal this information, simply state, *"Because I pay the premiums on this insurance, I am entitled to this information. I can either get it from you, or I can call the state banking commissioner and let them know that you refused to give me this information."* That should be all you need to do to get the information you want. If not, call your banking commissioner to complain. You can also call the well-known private mortgage insurance companies yourself, if you already know who holds your insurance. Here are seven of the most well-known companies, and their toll-free phone numbers:

GE Mortgage Insurance Corporation: 800/334-9270

Mortgage Guaranty Insurance Corporation (MGIC): 800/558-9900

PMI Mortgage Insurance Company: 800/288-1970

RADIAN Guaranty Corporation: 800/257-7643 or 800/523-1988

Republic Mortgage Insurance Company (RMIC): 800/999-7642

Triad Guaranty Insurance Corporation: 800/451-4872

United Guarantee Corporation: 800/334-8966

What If Your Lender Threatens To Foreclose?

There are ways to keep your house — or at least get out from under the mortgage debt — without having your home go through foreclosure. If you can't get assistance from your PMI company, call your lender's loss mitigation department. Tell your lender what is happening with your financial situation and ask for the name and address of the person you can submit a proposal to for a loan workout or a note modification agreement. These are just fancy terms for a proposal that lets you adjust the terms of your existing mortgage so you can afford to keep your home.

Here's one "workout" arrangement that will help if you fell one month behind on your mortgage and are now in a position to continue to pay your current month's mortgage, but can't bring that late payment up to date. Tell your lender that you can pay this month's mortgage, but that you don't have the resources to also pay the past due payment.

Tell your lender you need to spread the late payment out over 12 months, so you can get caught up. For example, if your current mortgage is $1,200, you would pay $1,300 ($1,200 plus $100, which is one-twelfth of your mortgage payment). Also, ask the lender if it's possible to waive the late payment fee as well. This way, you'll pay your current monthly mortgage plus one-twelfth of your monthly mortgage and you'll be caught up again within a year — without a negative mark on your credit report.

Then explore your options. If you could rent out your home, would the rental income cover the payments that need to be made to your mortgage lender? If you could arrange a land contract (with the help of a good real estate lawyer!), could you set up the contract so the buyer pays enough money down to cover the defaulted loan amount and taxes, plus enough of a monthly payment to cover what the lender needs?

Once the buyer pays 20% of the home's value, they can then refinance with a conventional loan and pay you off completely. You can then pay off the mortgage lender completely and you still have a good credit reference, instead of a foreclosure. And, if the buyer defaults, your mortgage loan will be current.

Our homes are our biggest purchase — which is why it's be pretty scary to deal with problems with our homes. If you find yourself strapped, your first commitment should be to pay for your daily living expenses — your housing, transportation, food and medications. Once those expenses are covered, you can turn your attention to your credit cards.

What To Do About Your Credit Cards

Usually, your credit card companies will not close your account as long as you continue to make some payment, and as long as you're not trying to charge anything more to the credit card. If you're not able to pay *anything* toward the balance due they will close your account or suspend your privileges. It looks better on your credit report if *you* close an account at your request, so if you find yourself in over your head and think you will miss payments, cut up the card and send it in with a letter of explanation, like this one, stating that you need to close this account while you catch up on your bills. This way, you don't put a new black mark on your newly cleaned credit report. (You'll see why I recommend using *secured* credit cards.)

(Date)

[Creditor]
[Address]
[City, State, Zip]
Re: [Your account number]

Dear Sir/Madam:

My financial situation has changed unexpectedly because [I was laid off, lost my job, had a medical crisis, was divorced, etc.].

I am writing to request that you close the above-referenced account <u>at my request</u> and use my secured savings deposit to pay off (or pay down) the balance on the account. I will then continue to make payments on the account until it is paid in full.

I look forward to being a customer of yours in the future. For now, however, I must ask you to close this account.

Thank you for your prompt attention to this matter.

Cordially,
[Your name]

If you run into a problem trying to get a creditor to honor your request to close your account and use your security deposit to pay off a portion of the balance (assuming that the creditor gave you a line of credit over and above your security deposit amount), your next step is the enforcement agency for that creditor. Send a copy of your letter, along with a letter stating that the creditor would not close your account as requested to: Division of Credit Practices, Bureau of Consumer Protection, FTC, 6th & Pennsylvania Avenue, NW, Washington, DC 20580

What To Do About Other Bills You Have

Here are five other types of bills that you can usually get an extension to pay without damaging your credit report:

1. *Utility companies.* Your local utility may be willing to work out a payment schedule for you for a short time. Just make sure you call them the minute you know you're going to be late. Don't put it off! Utilities won't generally show up on your credit report. However, if you pay late and wind up having your service temporarily shut off, you may need to pay the total balance in full *and* put up a security deposit for future service.

2. *Medical bills.* Most doctor, dentist and hospital bills won't usually be reported to credit bureaus unless the bills are sent to collections. Try to work out a modified payment schedule with your doctor before this happens. You can protect your credit r

report by asking your medical provider not to report your late status to your credit bureau as long as you're paying something each month. With medical bills, even a $5 payment each and every month will show your good faith effort to get the debts paid off.

3. *Gasoline cards.* Gasoline companies don't usually report your payment history unless your account falls delinquent 90 days or more. Again, you can usually work out a modified payment schedule to catch up if you fall behind. Just make sure you don't continue making charges to the credit card.

4. *Car payments.* Ask to skip a month on your car payments. Many lenders will let you skip one payment during the life of the car loan and tack it onto the back of the loan period. If you're going to be late or know you'll miss a payment, call the lender before they call you. You'll have much better luck working out arrangements *before* your payments are late instead of *after* they're late. In most cases, your lender will charge you a processing fee, which is usually 25% of your monthly payment. If they want to charge you much more than that, you're probably better off finding a way to make the entire car payment.

5. *Student loans.* With your student loans, first see about getting a deferment. If you're having financial difficulty because you've lost your job or been laid off, for example, most student loan organizations will give you a six month "unemployment deferment." If you do wind up missing a payment and you need to get caught up, talk with the lender.

For instance, once I'd gotten back on my feet, my remaining student loan payment was about $50 a month. When I was laid off from my job several years ago, I stayed current with my payments until my unemployment ran out, then I called and asked for a deferment. They gave me a six month deferment, but I was still behind one payment.

The nice thing about student loans is that you can make partial payments and get caught up. Once my deferment ended, I made one simple phone call and arranged to send in payments of $60 for five months...which got me caught up again. You can easily do the same thing.

If you know you'll have another bill paid off in six months, offer to pay half of your student loan payment for the next six months, then the full payment (which you can do using the additional money you were paying toward the other bill). If you start repaying your student loan regularly, and then find yourself falling behind, you may be able to get a lower payment worked out for a few months, until you're on your feet again.

If you're still having trouble getting your bills paid on time, you may need to use a credit or budget counselor.

What To Expect When You Use a Credit Counselor's Repayment Plan

With a credit or budget counselor, you set up a workable budget and send one lump sum payment to the credit counseling service so they can divide the money up among your creditors. You write one check to the credit counselor and they take the money and divide it up among your creditors. And, because you'll have learned some new money management strategies, there's a better chance that you'll stay out of debt, for good.

Most credit and budget counselors can work with your creditors to get them to accept smaller payments from you, and attempt to freeze or lower interest rates and late payment or over-the-limit fees. When you use a credit counselor, they can often stop the harassing phone calls from creditors that seem to come every ten minutes during dinner.

Credit counselors can only help if you have income to make payments to your creditors. Even part-time income will be enough to get you started. The required payments usually run about 3% of the debt, and are usually paid out over 36 months, much the same as a Chapter 13 bankruptcy.

Your credit counselor should be able to get your creditors to either immediately reduce their interest rates or get them reduced after you've made 3-6 months' worth of payments on time. Larger creditors, such as MBNA and Citibank — which often will only negotiate their interest rates if you're using a credit counseling service — are more likely to lower or freeze your interest rate immediately. If you stick with the program, your debts will be paid off within three years.

Some CCCS agencies report to the credit bureaus that your accounts are under repayment through them. As a result, some of your accounts will be listed on your credit report as "being paid under a repayment plan," but not all of them will be listed that way. The other credit counseling services don't report anything to the credit bureaus. Your creditors will generally only report that your account is being paid under a repayment plan if you're paying less than your normal minimum monthly payment or if your payments under the plan are paid to them late.

Many people who have used credit counselors have found that they've spent 3-6 months in the repayment plan before their accounts started being reported as up-to-date. Even so, many creditors don't even report this activity on your credit report.

Within 3-5 months of repayment through a good credit counselor, however, you should find your credit report in good standing.

Independent credit counselors are more likely to have your best interest at heart. CCCS, on the other hand, is set up to help both you and your creditors. Some offices are more consumer-friendly while others are more creditor-friendly. Shop around to find a credit counseling service that is willing to work with you on your behalf to try and get creditors to freeze or lower interest rates, remove late payment or over-the-limit penalties, and update your account's status on your credit reports.

It's better to show that you paid the account with budgeting help than to show that you were consistently late, or that the creditor charged off the account. Once you finish the repayment program, your accounts will be adjusted to show that your account was paid in full.

Selecting a Good Credit or Budget Counselor

If you do decide to use a credit counselor's debt repayment program, after you meet with the counselor for your free budget counseling session, ask for an experienced credit counselor. When credit counselors are first hired, they usually receive a few weeks of training, where they follow an experienced counselor around. Then the credit counselor starts the certification process, which takes two years. During those two years, the credit counselor will be tested on material from various study guides, which covers things like counseling psychology, consumer rights and collection practices.

As a result, a new counselor may not yet have any experience or knowledge about a particular problem you may be having.

Your financial future is too important to put in the hands of an inexperienced counselor. Ask to be assigned to a counselor who has at least two years of experience. Then, once you get your counselor, be sure to ask these questions before you sign up:

1. *Which of my creditors have worked with you in the past to reduce payments, or freeze or lower interest and fees?* Before you sign up for a repayment plan, make sure that the counseling service can help you reduce interest and fees for *your* creditors. Not all creditors are willing to negotiate with credit counselors. If most or all of your creditors *are* willing to negotiate, then it may be in your best interest to start a repayment plan. If most of your creditors won't work with the credit counselor, then a repayment plan won't work for you. To be on the safe side, ask the credit counselor for a list of the creditors that have worked with them or have them put in writing which of your creditors they have successfully negotiated with in the past. These creditors often work with credit counselors: *American Express, AT&T, Bank One, Bank of America, Citibank, Crestar Bank, Capital One, Discover, First Union, First USA, GE Capital, JC Penney, MBNA, Sears and USAA.*

2. *Can you take money electronically out of my checking account or will I have to send you a certified check or money order each month?* You're much more likely to stick with a repayment plan if making the payment is a "no-brainer." If you're pressed for time and don't think you can get to your bank each month to get a certified check, make sure the counseling service can take money out of your account electronically.

3. *When will my creditors be paid?* Some counseling services have a set date each month when they take money out and apply it to your debts. Sometimes, creditors wind up being paid after their due dates. Make sure that the counseling service will work with your creditors to change the due dates or will set up

your payment schedule based on when you get paid. The best services will work around your payday *and* your bills' due dates.

4. *How often can I see statements of my accounts?* Your counselor should send you monthly reports showing you how much of your payment is going toward interest, how much toward the minimum payment and how much toward the counselor for his/her services. Generally, expect to pay around $15 to get started and $3 a month for each creditor. If you're paying much more than that, the counselor isn't doing you a service. After you've been with the program 3-6 months, request a copy of your credit reports and double check that the creditors are reporting your account the way the counselor said they would.

5. *Do I have to put all of my debts on the repayment plan or only some?* Accounts that have low balances or accounts that you're current on don't need to be listed in the repayment plan, unless you want them to be. Don't let a credit counselor strong-arm you into putting all the debts onto the repayment plan unless you believe it's the only way you'll get them paid off.

6. *Will I always deal with the same counselor, or at least get a live person on the phone when I call during regular business hours? How long does it take for you to return phone calls?* Make sure you're comfortable with the answers you get here, and that you're comfortable with the people you might be dealing with. After your free budget counseling session, call your counselor once or twice with questions you have about the budget paperwork to make sure that you don't have a problem getting your questions answered and your phone calls returned.

Choosing the Best Credit or Budget Counselor For Your Needs

Choosing the best credit or budget counselor for your needs is a lot like choosing the best secured credit card. There is no one best counselor for everyone. The best counselor for you will depend on your needs. Individual counselors, or prosperity advisors such as myself, work well if you need hands-on guidance — but they will also expect you to be actively involved in getting out from under your debt.

For instance, I encourage people I counsel to make a commitment to themselves to not add any new debt, one day at a time. I also encourage them to change the way they think about debt and money, explore and expand their money beliefs so they start getting rid of negative thoughts and actions about money, and start filling their lives with more positive thoughts and actions about money. And I have them use my *GoalGetting Strategy* in Chapter 3, to get focused on what they want to achieve in life. That's a lot of work!

If you're up for the task, you can get additional information on my counseling services by calling 800-507-9244. I charge $50/hour to help you work out a repayment plan that fits your family's income and to help you create a permanent prosperity consciousness.

If you prefer a larger, more traditional credit counseling agency, there are four different organizations that I recommend. There's no obligation or payment due to any of these groups until *after* you've determined what your monthly payment would be under the plan *and* you've joined their program. I encourage you to explore all your options and then pick the one you're most comfortable with.

Consumer Credit Counseling Service (CCCS; 800/388-2227). CCCS has local offices across the country and the 800-number will automatically connect you to the office nearest you. The quality of service (and the cost) varies at each site, but you can generally get good budgeting help at CCCS. If the counselor tells you that bankruptcy is your only option, try the other organizations listed here first before you take that step. If you'd like an ongoing relationship with your counselor, where you can sit down face-to-face every few weeks, this is the group for you.

Readers have reported excellent service from the CCCS in Houston, Texas. Less than stellar reports have come in regarding the Budget Credit Counseling Service in New York City. If you wind up using CCCS, please write me and let me know how your experience is — good, bad or indifferent!

MyVesta.org (formerly Debt Counselors of America; 800/680-3328). MyVesta is a non-profit which is funded primarily by donations from consumers. They ask for an initial tax-deductible donation of $50 (which you pay only after you agree on a monthly payment amount), and charge $2.90 per creditor each month. When the counselors review your debts they'll tell you if you have creditors that won't negotiate with them. MyVesta pays creditors weekly, and your monthly payment to MyVesta is due the 15th of each month. MyVestsa also has a very comprehensive secure website (http://www.MyVesta.org) where you can view your account statements whenever you like.

Genus Credit Management (formerly National Credit Counseling Service/NCCS; 888/844-6227). Genus is the nation's largest non-profit credit counseling organization and offers 24-hour service, Monday through Saturday. Sunday hours are 9am-6pm. They also have a website at http://www.genus.org. Genus charges $2 per creditor each month. With Genus your payment can be directly deducted from your checking account on any day of the month. Your creditors are paid monthly but Genus tries to match up your payment date with your due dates so your bills get paid on time. Genus offers immediate assistance by phone, rather than local appointments. This is handy if you're in a time crunch and need to set up a repayment plan immediately or if you'd prefer to remain anonymous. If in-person contact with your counselor is important to you, you may prefer CCCS.

Lawyers United For Debt Relief (LUDR, 800/992-3275, Ext. 2). LUDR (www.ludr.org) is the place to go if you can't even pay your creditors the minimums due — or if you're behind on your car or mortgage. While your fee each month is more expensive (the first payment to set up the program, then 10% of your monthly payment, which averages out to $26/month), what you get is a debtors' rights attorney working on your behalf to negotiate with your creditors and get them to stop foreclosure, repossession or garnishments — and get them to lower the minimum payment. They can also help you refinance defaulted student loans at an interest rate of 8.25%, so long as the loans are not already involved in a court case.

Once you complete your repayment program with a credit counselor, get copies of your credit reports again. Then use the strategies in Chapter 2 to make sure that all the accounts included in the repayment program are being reported accurately. Sometimes your credit reports will show that you're still in a debt repayment or debt management program. Other times, your credit reports will show that you still have past due bills, even though those are the bills you just paid off. Check out your credit reports and take whatever steps you need to take to update your credit report so it still shows you in the best light possible.

What If You Have To Declare Bankruptcy Again

Sometimes, declaring bankruptcy causes more problems than it solves. Some of us just aren't ready to be debt-free and may not know how to live without debt. Or circumstances outside of your control may put you in a position where you can't pay your debts again. As a result, you may find yourself so seriously in debt again that you're faced with the hardest decision of all: Should you declare bankruptcy again?

First, I recommend that you use all the strategies in this chapter to see if there's any way you can get back on your feet again. Re-read the reaffirmation section of Chapter 2, in case you opted to continue paying on a debt that you might have been better off discharging the first time around.

Today, you have the capability to decide what you want to do. Should you seek credit counseling? Should you declare Chapter 13 bankruptcy and try and repay your bills? If you can't keep up with your Chapter 13 payments, should you declare Chapter 7? Should you set up a strict budget to pay down the bills and tighten the belts until they are all paid off? Only you will know which decisions you are up to, emotionally. And what you decide WILL BE THE BEST DECISION FOR YOU. It's okay if you feel embarrassed about having to declare bankruptcy again, but look at it this way. The bankruptcy protection laws exist to help you get back on your feet. Yes, you made some mistakes. But now you're taking steps to get back on track.

Declaring bankruptcy again is a perfectly acceptable way to grab the bull by the horns and take action to get your finances under control. It will all be okay, I promise. If you find yourself waking up at night, or unable to sleep because of anxiety and worries about having to declare bankruptcy again, stop yourself wherever you are. Take a deep breath right then and there and say to yourself, at least 10 times: "I am doing the right thing. I am doing what is best for me, my family and our future."

What If You Declared Chapter 7 Bankruptcy
Within the Past Six Years

If it's been less than six years since you declared Chapter 7 bankruptcy and you still can't get out from under your debts, or you've fallen behind on your mortgage, car payments, alimony, child support or taxes, then you may need to declare Chapter 13 bankruptcy. Unlike your Chapter 7 bankruptcy, a Chapter 13 bankruptcy allows you to set up a repayment plan for your creditors and will help you prevent or postpone a foreclosure on your home, or repossession of your car.

When you file a Chapter 7 to discharge whatever debts you can, and then file a Chapter 13 to help you set up a payment plan to repay your remaining debts, it is commonly referred to by bankruptcy attorneys as "filing a Chapter 20." There's no such thing as a Chapter 20, of course, but it's becoming a more common technique that people are using when they are still over their head in debt. You may find yourself in this situation if a creditor pressured you to reaffirmed a debt that would have been dischargeable, or if you haven't successfully changed your money attitudes and habits.

What If You Declared Chapter 13 Bankruptcy
and You're Still in Repayment

Your Chapter 13 repayment plan was originally set up for three to five years. Don't be discouraged if you aren't able to keep up with your payments — only 25% of the people who declare Chapter 13 ever finish their repayment plans. Some have their Chapter 13 bankruptcy dismissed when they're finally able to sell their homes. Others simply can't keep up with their payments. If money is really tight in your Chapter 13 repayment plan, first see if there are any effortless ways you can generate some income that you could use to accelerate the payoff of one of your larger debts (like your car loan) to get extra money each month.

Could you rent out a room? Rent out space in the garage to someone working on an antique car? Could you sell extra television sets, or other old stuff you haven't used in a year? Sit down and brainstorm ways you can free up some money each month. Even if you take clothes to a consignment shop and get an extra $16 for your effort, that's $16 you could put toward your next car payment — or $16 you could use as extra spending money. The choice is yours.

If all else fails, and you find that you simply cannot keep up with your Chapter 13 repayment plan, you have three choices:

1. You can talk with your trustee about either extending your payment period to five years (if it's not already five years), or working out lower payments under your existing repayment plan.

2. Depending on the circumstances, ou can have your Chapter 13 dismissed and refile a new Chapter 13 and start the repayment process again.

3. You can convert your Chapter 13 to a Chapter 7. The drawback to this situation is that you may have debts that won't be discharged under the Chapter 7. You will either have to give up these items or pay off the debts directly to the creditors.

If you believe that declaring bankruptcy again may be your only option, go see two or three bankruptcy attorneys — including your original attorney if you like — and explore your options. When you're looking for a good attorney, start by looking to see if there are any Board Certified bankruptcy attorneys in your area. There are fewer than 300 certified bankruptcy attorneys in the country, so don't be too alarmed if you can't find one near you — but it's certainly a bonus if you can.

Certified attorneys spend hundreds of hours in extra training, to make sure they meet your needs as well as possible. They also have years of experience, have to pass a comprehensive exam on consumer bankruptcy, and meet the highest legal and ethical standards. You can get a free referral to local certified bankruptcy attorneys from the American Bankruptcy Board of Certification (ABBC) which is a division of the American Bankruptcy Institute (ABI). You can reach ABBC at 703/739-0800.

Once you decide to go ahead with a particular attorney, contact all of your creditors and tell them that you're declaring bankruptcy. Simply say, *"I'm retaining an attorney and the bankruptcy court will contact you as soon as my paperwork is filled out."* This way, your lawyer doesn't have to spend time fielding calls from creditors and your creditors will know that they are waiting for your bankruptcy paperwork to be ready.

As soon as your bankruptcy is discharged, start at the beginning of this book and follow the recommended strategies so you can make sure you don't wind up in this situation again.

Chapter 10: Action Items

1. Use any short-term strategies you can to reduce your expenses and pay off your debts.

2. Seriously consider going to at least three different Debtors' Anonymous meetings to find support with others who are having problems controlling their spending.

3. Take the quiz to see if you have a gambling problem.

4. Contact your creditors if you're falling behind on your payments.

5. Take steps to protect your home if you fall behind on your mortgage.

6. Set up a repayment plan you can afford with each of your creditors.

7. Close credit card accounts if you need to.

8. See a budget or credit counselor.

9. See at least three attorneys if you think you have to declare bankruptcy again.

10. Reread this book and put the strategies to use for you!

chapter 11

Building Financial Security

In this chapter, I'm going to give you a few advanced money-saving strategies that you can use to build a rock-solid financial foundation.

Investing Your Money Once You're Out of Debt

Following the *DebtBuster Strategies* in Chapter 2, you can start rebuilding your financial future by paying off any debts that aren't listed on your bankruptcy. Then, as you pay off these debts, you can use the money you now have available to increase your savings. For example, once you pay off any student loan you have, you can start investing that money into a mutual fund.

Invesco (800/525-8085) and *American Century Investments* (800/345-2021) both have good money market and stock mutual funds that will help you build up sizable savings over the next five to ten years. If you can put away $150 a month, that's $1,800 a year you'll be saving. And that money can grow year after year, by 5% or more.

Prepay Big Loans And Save Thousands In Interest

The second advanced strategy I want to share with you is prepayment of your large loans — your car loans and your mortgage. Prepaying large loans can really save you some hefty interest. For example, my car loan was $239 a month. I paid $250 every month and paid off my loan two months early.

You can do the same thing with your mortgage. Look at your mortgage statement to see how much of your payment is interest and how much is principal. Make your regular payment and include an extra principal payment of $50-$100. You can save tens of thousands of dollars over the course of your loan. Even if you only stay in your house a few years, those extra principal payments work to your advantage because you'll have that much more equity built up in your home when you sell.

Don't pay the $300-$500 fee your mortgage company charges when they offer to set up an automatic payment plan for you. Keep control of the payments yourself. This way, if you ever need that extra $100 for something else one month, you're not locked into paying it toward your mortgage.

Best Ways To Prepay Your Mortgage

What's the best way to prepay your mortgage? The absolute smartest way to prepay your mortgage is to divide one month's payment by 12 and add that amount to the amount you pay you every month.

Write down your monthly mortgage amount: $_____. Now, divide that amount by 12 and write that amount here: $_____. Add the two numbers together and you'll know how much to pay each month. For example, if your monthly mortgage is $600, you would pay $600 plus $600/12 ($50) = $650.

The extra money you pay goes to reduce your principal. After 12 months of paying an extra $50, you've actually paid an entire extra year's worth of your mortgage. That's because for the first 15 yeras of a 30-year mortgage, only about $50 of your current mortgage actually goes toward paying down the principal of your loan — the rest goes toward paying interest. The more money you send, over and above your monthly payment, the sooner you pay off your mortgage.

If you don't think you've got the discipline to always send in that extra amount, then you might want to look into setting up a bi-weekly mortgage, where half of your mortgage gets taken out of your checking account every two weeks. This way, instead of making 12 monthly payments, you make 13 payments during the year. You can save yourself tens of thousands of dollars if you prepay your mortgage using a bi-weekly mortgage. Let's assume you have a 30-year, $100,000 mortgage, at 8.5%. After paying every month for ten years, using the conventional method, you'll have only paid off $11,399 of your loan and will still owe $90,000.

Pay your mortgage over ten years using bi-weekly payments, however, and you'll have paid off $23,242 — building up nearly twice the equity in the same amount of time. In addition, you'll cut nearly eight years off the life of your loan — you'll have completely paid off that $100,000 mortgage within 22.6 years. And you'll have saved yourself over $50,000 in interest. I can think of a whole lot better things to do with $50,000 than lining my mortgage lender's pocket, can't you?

Ten Strategies To Help You Avoid Money Drains

Once you've finished saving money on your big expenses, look a little closer at the everyday things you enjoy, whether they're for fun or necessity. Cable television, mail order clubs, utilities and car maintenance: they all cost money, even if only a little. When you add them up at the end of the month, you'll discover extra padding that you can strip away — without stripping away your enjoyment of them. You wind up with more money and you don't have to scrimp.

1. *Only order cable TV premium channels on sale.* Don't pay monthly rates for premium channels unless the cable company is offering a special deal. Premium channels can cost $10 a month — or more. However, cable companies often offer 6-month specials, where you can get two premium channels for the price of one. Keep tabs on your cable bill and cancel channels when the special offer expires. You won't always have the same premium channels each month, but variety is good for your soul!

2. *Check out the pay-per-view channels, which let you decide which programs are worth paying for.* Titles and prices of movies, sporting events, and other programming are listed in your TV guide. When a program catches your eye, order it by calling the telephone number listed on the screen and giving the program's order number. Viola!

3. *See matinees.* With movie ticket prices at $6-$8, treating yourself to a movie — not to a mention treating your whole family — can cost you a small fortune. You don't have to stop going to the movies. Go to the matinee instead. On weekdays and weekends, ticket prices are often half price before 6 p.m. Also, some theaters offer discounts for students and senior citizens. Look in the phone book for theaters that charge $1.50/or $0.99 for tickets. Your employer's Human Relations office may also offer free movie tickets — call them and ask.

4. *Rent movies.* If you have a VCR, wait for movies to come out on video. Your family can watch a movie (and have popcorn and root beer floats) for about $4. Make sure you

return the tape on time. It was actually cheaper to order several movie channels when I lived in the boonies and didn't return tapes on time. Nothing brings you back to earth quicker than a $30 video store bill.

5. *Never order your bank checks from your bank.* Order your checks directly from a check company — not your bank. Banks act as the middleman between you and the check company, and they charge you $9-$15 for the service. Go straight to the same source your bank uses. It's a lot cheaper. Some reputable check companies include *Checks in the Mail* (800/733-4443), *Checks Unlimited by Current Inc.* (800/533-3973) and the *Check Gallery* (800/354-3540). You can get 100 checks for under $5.

6. *Cancel — or avoid "clubs."* Don't join video, record, CD or book "clubs" that send you catalogs. These catalog companies are money-sinkholes designed to convince you to spend money. And these sales pitches work, too. They know that keeping an item you don't really want is easier than re-packing it.

7. *Pare down your magazine subscriptions.* Subscribe only to the magazines you read cover to cover every time you get them. Those are the ones that give you your money's worth. If you find magazines laying on the coffee table, still wrapped in plastic with their pages flawlessly uncrumpled, cancel your subscription right away and get your money back. Those $9.95 (or more) subscriptions add up! Pick up individual issues of that magazine or read them at the library.

8. *Keep your miscellaneous food purchases in check.* Going out to a restaurant means no cooking and no cleaning, but it's expensive — especially if you do it often. Cook at home as often as you can. Pack lunch; bring a thermos to work if you don't like the office brew. Buy your own Snickers stash for work — it's a lot

cheaper. The same goes for soda — a 2-liter bottle in the office fridge (bought on sale) costs you less money than two cans of soda. I easily spent $10 a day on drinks, snacks and lunch — that's $200 a month spent on overpriced food that didn't go very far. Half that amount spent on the same grocery store items could have kept me well-fed and $100 richer, every month.

9. *Maintain your car*. Regular oil changes are a must. Don't wait until your car breaks down to get something fixed or a little gremlin of a problem will grow into a monster. Clip coupons for the garage you regularly use — or see if your local garage has a frequent customer's club, where you can usually get one free oil change after your sixth oil change.

10. *Use smart energy-saving techniques*. Utilities are a huge drain to your wallet. Dripping faucets, running the heat on tropical in the winter and the air-conditioning on subarctic in the summer are all money drains. Be comfortable in your home but keep an even temperature. Don't open the refrigerator all the time. Join local utility energy-saving programs that cycle you on and off during peak periods and save $8 a month effortlessly.

Chapter 11: Action Items

1. Call several mutual fund families and get information on investing in your future.

2. Set up a prepayment plan for your mortgage that you can live with.

3. Each month use a strategy to avoid money drains — and brainstorm with your family to come up with more great ways to effortlessly save money!

chapter 12

Keep Up The Good Work!

Congratulations! You've now spent about 40 hours of your time and energy fixing your financial problems. That week's worth of time is already showing results for you. Keep up the good work even if you feel like you're spinning your wheels, on any particular day. Keep saving a little money every day.

Four Strategies To Keep You On Track

Here are a few final ways to keep on the right track:

1. *Pay your bills on time.* Mark on your calendar the day your bills are due, and the day you need to mail them to arrive on time (give yourself a good week to avoid late payment fees and finance charges). Or use a computer program like *Quicken*, *Microsoft Money* or *The Budget Kit.*

2. *Choose your expenses carefully.* If you don't need something, don't buy it — even if it's on sale. Treat yourself with something you really need, saving up for it first so you can pay for it in cash to avoid running up your credit card. Separate the necessities from the luxuries (no matter how small). One of my happiest "treats" was an easy-to-use, $9.95 manual can opener.

3. *Balance your checkbook.* The first time one woman finally got up the nerve to balance her checkbook she found a $50 error — in *her* favor! Know how much money you've spent

and how much you've deposited — and make sure you always deposit more than you spend. You can avoid having any bounced check charges eat away at your earning power if you make a commitment to yourself not to "float" checks, writing them out before the money is in your account.

4. *Take care of problems before they occur or as they occur.* Don't wait for problems to explode into costly and stressful disasters. Whether it's a problem with a credit bureau, paying a bill, whatever, get help.

Good Resources To Check Out

"2000 Consumer's Resource Handbook." *U.S. Office of Consumer Affairs. Washington, DC*

Directory of Companies Offering Dividend Reinvestment Plans, 15th Edition. *Laurel, Maryland: Evergreen Enterprises, 1998.*

"How to Dispute Credit Report Errors" *Public Reference, Federal Trade Commission, Washington, DC 20580.*

"Settlement Costs: A HUD Guide; Revised Edition" *U.S. Department of Housing and Urban Development, 451 Seventh Street, SW, Washington, DC 20410; 202/708-4560, Free.*

Ban Breathnach, Sarah. Simple Abundance: A Daybook of Comfort and Joy. *New York: Warner, 1995.*

Caher, James P. and John M. Debt Free: Your Guide to Personal Bankruptcy Without Shame. *New York: Henry Holt, 1996.*

Dolan, Ken and Daria. Smart Money: How to Be Your Own Financial Manager. *New York: Berkeley Books, 1990.*

Dominguez, Joe and Vicki Robin. Your Money Or Your Life. *New York: Penguin, 1992.*

Feinberg, Andrew. Downsize Your Debt: How to Take Control Of Your Personal Finances. *New York: Penguin Books, 1993.*

Horowitz, Shel. The Penny Pinching Hedonist. *Mass: AWM, 1995.*

Jaffe, Azriela. Create Your Own Luck. *Mass.: Adams Media, 2000.*

Knouse, Ken. True Prosperity: Your Guide to a Cash-Based Lifestyle. *Texas: Double-Dome, 1996.*

Lawrence, Judy. The Budget Kit: The Common Cents Money Management Workbook. *Chicago: Dearborn, 2000.*

Lawrence, Judy. Money Tracker. *Chicago: Dearborn, 1996.*

Leonard, Robin. Money Trouble: Legal Strategies to Cope With Your Debt. *Berkeley, California: Nolo Press, 1993.*

McWilliams, Peter and John-Roger. Wealth 101: Getting What You Want — Enjoying What You've Got. *Los Angeles: Prelude Press, 1992.*

Mundis, Jerrold. How to Get Out of Debt, Stay Out of Debt and Live Prosperously. *New York: Bantam, 1988.*

Mundis, Jerrold. Making Peace With Money. *Kansas City: Andrews McMeel, 1999.*

Ponder, Catherine. The Dynamic Laws of Prosperity. *Marina del Rey, California: DeVorss & Company, 1993.*

Ponder, Catherine. The Prosperity Secrets of the Ages. *Marina del Rey, California: DeVorss & Company, 1986.*

Ponder, Catherine. Open Your Mind to Prosperity. *Marina del Rey, California: DeVorss & Company, 1984.*

Ponder, Catherine. Open Your Mind to Receive. *Marina del Rey, California: DeVorss & Company, 1983.*

Ponder, Catherine. The Secret of Unlimited Prosperity. *Marina del Rey, California: DeVorss & Company, 1981.*

Ponder, Catherine. Dare to Prosper! *Marina del Rey, California: DeVorss & Company, 1983.*

Ponder, Catherine. The Prospering Power of Love. *Marina del Rey, California: DeVorss & Company, 1984.*

Ponder, Catherine. The Prospering Power of Prayer. *Marina del Rey, California: DeVorss & Company, 1983.*

Remele, Patricia. Money Freedom: Finding Your Inner Source Of Wealth. *Virginia Beach: ARE Press, 1995.*

Ross, Ruth. Prospering Woman: A Complete Guide to Achieving the Full, Abundant Life. *San Rafael, California: New World Library, 1995.*

A Final Word From the Author

I hope you feel that this book has helped you reclaim your financial security. The nicest thing about the work I do with **my seminars, on-line newsletter, financial columns and America On-Line's** personal finance forum is that people often send me email letting me know how they're progressing.

Please write me and let me know how things are going for you! You can send a letter via snail mail to me through my publisher at Pellingham Casper Communications, Prosperity Books & Seminars, 1121 Annapolis Road, Suite 120, Odenton, MD 21113. Or you reach me via email at: PaulaRyan@ArtOfAbundance.com.

Do you have other strategies that helped you get back on your feet after bankruptcy? Have you run into a snag trying to use one of the enclosed strategies? Have you come across any credit offers that are outrageous scams or really great secured cards? Do you have a prosperity story you'd like to share with me? I'd love to hear about your experiences and hear how your progress is coming along. One person at a time, we can stop being victims of creditor and start being in charge of our own financial future.

I enjoy the time I spend helping people *Bounce Back From Bankruptcy* and *Break the Debt Cycle For Good!*. I've also really enjoyed getting to know my readers better — and learning more about their experiences as they've rebuilt their lives after declaring bankruptcy. I hope you'll send me a letter and a picture so I can visualize you and your new prosperity. I wish you the best of luck with your financial freedom!

Peace and prosperity,
Paula Langguth Ryan
October, 2000

About the Author

Paula Langguth Ryan is a Contemporary Prosperity Advisor, financial columnist and motivational speaker. As such, she is devoted to giving people the resources they need to change the way they think and feel about money — so they can achieve personal prosperity and abundance in all areas of their lives. She accomplishes this goal through her groundbreaking seminars, in-service workshops, sermons, lessons, articles, books and tapes.

Her seminars and lessons, now available on tape, include:
Break the Debt Cycle — For Good! (60 minutes)
How to Become a Money Magnet (60 minutes)
Embracing Abundance (20 minutes)
Creating a Prosperity Consciousness in Everyday Life (20 minutes)

Other seminars and workshops include:
Mastering the Art of Unconditional Receiving
Money Really Does Grow on Trees!
The Secret to Getting the Goals You Set
Bounce Back From Bankruptcy
Treasure Mapping 101
A Radical, Prosperous Approach to Debt Collection
Ten Tips to Break the Debt Cycle
How to Help Your Clients Travel Without Credit

Ms. Ryan's twice-monthly prosperity e-zine, *The Art of Abundance*, is available by sending an email to PaulaRyan@ArtOfAbundance.com.

For more information about the above titles, to find out about upcoming seminars in your area, or to schedule Ms. Ryan as a speaker for your school, business, organization or religious institution, call 800-507-9244 or write Prosperity Books & Seminars, 1121 Annapolis Road, Suite 120, Odenton, MD 21113 or fax 775-201-6705.

> ### Visit Paula's Website at
> ### ww.ArtOfAbundance.com

Excerpt from the forthcoming
Break the Debt Cycle -- For Good!
by Paula Langguth Ryan

In these pages, you'll discover specific strategies to help you get out of debt, stay out of debt and change the way you think about money. You really need to change the way you think about money on an internal level, becauase that's the only way you're going to be able to break the debt cycle for good.

Everything you've ever learned about money, you learned by the time you were five years old. Think back for a minute about how your parents dealt with money. What would your parents say when you wanted something?

Do these phrases sound familiar? *We can't afford it. You don't need it. Money doesn't grow on trees. I'm not made of money. There's not enough. You can't have everything you want.* Do you recognize your parents in these phrases?

Just like our parents, we've bought into the idea that money is good or bad, that money has the ability to control how you feel, what you can do or not do, what you can have or not have, who you can be or not be.

The truth is, money is energy. Nothing more and nothing less. And there is an infinite supply of energy available. The Law of Conservation of Energy states it clearly: All matter is energy. And energy can neither be lost nor destroyed. It is merely converted.

You take your work energy and it is converted into pay-check energy, which is converted into grocery money energy, which is converted into food energy, which is converted into fuel for your body, which is converted into your work energy.

What you decide to do with your energy is up to you. How you decide to "spend" that energy, is up to you. The bottom line is that you *can* have anything you want. You just can't have *everything* all at one time.

The most important first step you can take to break the debt cycle for good is to decide for yourself what you truly *want* in life. The strategies in this book will help you discover what you truly want to be, do and have in your life. Once you decide what you truly want in life, you will start to make choices, based on what you truly want in life.

One choice you may make is that you will not take on any new unsecured debt, *today.* Just for today. Whatever happens, you will not add any new debt to the money you currently owe. You *can* make ends meet without taking on any new debt today.

What does that mean? What does no new debt mean? That means when someone says, "Hey, let's go to lunch!" You say, "That's okay, I brown-bagged it today." They say they're going to the new restaurant, it will be fun, come on. Your next immediate response might be "I really can't afford it." (Because that's our programmed response.) They're not deterred, "Don't worry about it, I'll front you."

Don't give in. This is your plan. Stay on course. You are not going to take on any new debt today. It means no buy now, pay later plans, it means no ordering something in the mail now becuase you know you'll have the money when the item comes. It means no writing the check for something on Friday because you know the money will be in the checking account on Monday. Take control of your money. Don't take on any new debt today.

Throughout this book, you'll find strategies to help you get through the tight weeks, so that you can keep this commitment to yourself to not take on any new debt today.

Harnessing the Prospering Power of Ten

The metaphysical prosperity principle of the Power of Ten has been around for ages. Harnessing the prospering power of ten begins with the money you have in your life right now.

You need to be grateful for what you have right now. See whatever you do have coming back to you tenfold. If you don't see yourself having enough money in your account to pay a particular bill that's due, for example, send what you can and see this money coming back to you tenfold, because you've freely given what you do have.

Harnessing the prospering power of your money means harnessing and directing your money's energy. We'll talk about this a great deal more, as we get further into the book, but it's important that you take this first step toward harnessing the prospering power of ten if you want to break the debt cycle for good.

You're going to have to change the way you think and feel about money if you want to truly break the debt cycle habit. It's not always easy, but it is incredibly rewarding. You can take big steps or small steps, breaking out of your comfort level one little inch at a time, until you've created new ways of thinking and feeling about money that support your goals. Now's the time for you to take charge of your financial future...are you ready?